1978

PEOPLES OF THE EARTH

volume seven

Andes

THE DANBURY PRESS

(Preceding page) Wildlife on Lake Titicaca is endangered as local Aymara tear totoa reeds from the banks — habitat of many species of bird. The reeds have always been used locally for boat building; now they are sold all over Peru for thatch and cattle fodder.

The publishers gratefully acknowledge help from the following organizations:
Royal Anthropological Institute, London
Musée de l'Homme, Paris
International African Institute, London
British Museum, London
Royal Geographical Society, London
Scott Polar Research Institute, Cambridge
Royal Asiatic Society, London
Royal Central Asian Society, London
Pitt-Rivers Museum, Oxford
Horniman Museum, London
Institute of Latin American Studies, London

The DANBURY PRESS
a division of GROLIER ENTERPRISES INC.
Publisher
ROBERT B. CLARKE

© 1973 Europa Verlag

Library of Congress Catalog Card No. 72 85614

Printed in Italy by
Arnoldo Mondadori Editore, Verona

Editorial Director **Tom Stacey**

Picture Director **Alexander Low**
Executive Editor **Katherine Ivens**
Art Director **Tom Deas**
Assistant Editor **Elisabeth Meakin**
Project Co-ordinator **Anne Harrison**
Research **Cheryl Moyer**
Specialist Picture Research **Claire Waterson**
Picture Research **Claire Baines**
Elly Beintema
Diana Eggitt
Jeanne Griffiths
Editorial Assistants **Richard Carlisle**
Rosamund Ellis
Susan Rutherford
Xan Smiley
Design Assistants **Susan Forster**
Richard Kelly
Cartography **Ron Hayward**
Illustrations **Sandra Archibald**
Ron McTrusty

Production **Roger Multon**

PHOTOGRAPHIC CREDITS
Cover – **Loren McIntyre, Romano Cagnoni, Mario de Biasi** (Epoca), **Foto Hetzel** (Claire Waterson), **David Drew Zingg** (Peter H. Schub), **Richard Harrington** (Camera Press). 2, 3 – **Tony Morrison** (Keystone Press). 14 through 23 – **Loren McIntyre**. 24, 25 – **Romano Cagnoni**. 27 – **Fred Maroon** (Louis Mercier). 28 – **Cornell Capa** (Magnum from the John Hillelson Agency). 28, 29 – **Claire Waterson**. 30 – **B. Smith, Foto Hetzel** (both Claire Waterson). 31 – **Mario de Biasi** (Epoca). 32, 33 – **Raymond Depardon** (John Hillelson Agency), **Romano Cagnoni, Fred J. Maroon** (Louis Mercier), **Claus Meyer** (Black Star). 34, 35 – **Foto Hetzel, Reflejo** (Claire Waterson). 36 through 43 – **Mario de Biasi** (Epoca). 44 through 48 – **Brian Moser** (Anglo Colombian Recording Expedition) exc. top and bot. lt. 48 – **Loren McIntyre**. 50 through 61 – **Victor Englebert**. 62 – **Foto Hetzel** (Claire Waterson). 63 through 65 – **Victor Englebert**. 66 – Tony Morrison (Keystone Press). 70 – **W. Bonnatti** (Epoca). 71 – **Foto Hetzel** (Claire Waterson). 72 – **Tony Morrison** (Keystone Press). 73 – **Cornell Capa** (Magnum from the John Hillelson Agency), **Reflejo** (Claire Waterson). 74 through 76 – **Reflejo, B. Smith, Foto Hetzel** (all Claire Waterson), **Claire Waterson**. 77 – **Marion Morrison** (Keystone Press), **Foto Hetzel** (Claire Waterson). 78 – **W. Bonatti** (Epoca). 79 – **Claire Waterson**. 80, 81 – **Victor Englebert**. 82, 83 – **Tony Morrison** (Keystone Press) exc. 83 bot. lt. (2) – **Victor Englebert**. 84, 85 – **Victor Englebert**. 86 – **P. Braun, Loren McIntyre, Victor Englebert, Tony Morrison** (Keystone Press). 88, 89 – **Victor Englebert**. 90 – Tony Morrison (Keystone Press), bot. lt. **Claire Waterson**. 91 – **Victor Englebert**. 92 – **Picturepoint**, bot. – **Claire Waterson**. 93 – **Foto Hetzel** (Claire Waterson). 94, 95 – **Tony Morrison** (Keystone Press). 96 – **Loren McIntyre, Claire Waterson, B. Smith** (Claire Waterson). 98 through 103 – **Tony Morrison** (Keystone Press). 104 through 107 – **Loren McIntyre** exc. top rt. 107 – **Reflejo** (Claire Waterson). 108 – **Loren McIntyre**. 110 through 119 – **David Drew Zingg** (Peter H. Schub). 121 – **Richard Harrington** (Camera Press). 122, 123 – **Sergio Larrain** (The John Hillelson Agency). 124, 125 – **Mike Andrews** (Daily Telegraph. 126 – **Davis Pratt** (Rapho, New York). 127 through 129 – **Mike Andrews** (Daily Telegraph) exc. top rt. 127 – **Sergio Larrain** (The John Hillelson Agency).

Contents

Supervisory Editor of the Series:
Professor Sir Edward Evans-Pritchard,
Fellow of All Souls, Professor of Social Anthropology,
University of Oxford, 1946-1970,
Chevalier de la Légion d'Honneur

Volume Editor: Dr Peter Rivière, University lecturer in Anthropology, Oxford, author of *Marriage Among the Trio: A Principle of Social Organization* etc

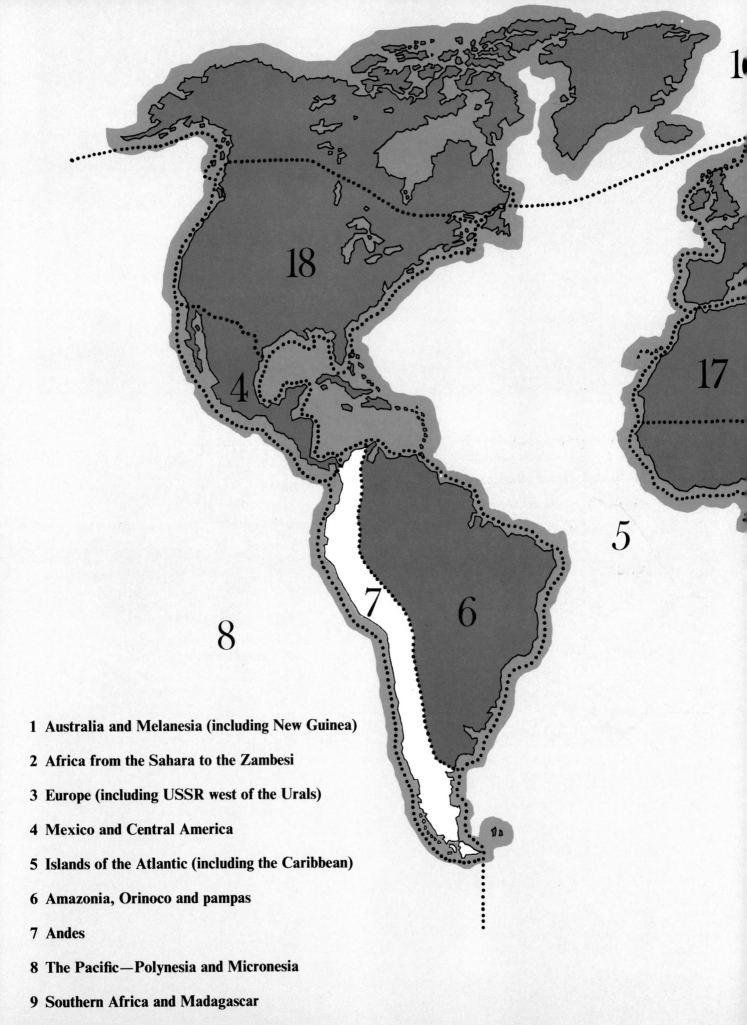

1   **Australia and Melanesia (including New Guinea)**

2   **Africa from the Sahara to the Zambesi**

3   **Europe (including USSR west of the Urals)**

4   **Mexico and Central America**

5   **Islands of the Atlantic (including the Caribbean)**

6   **Amazonia, Orinoco and pampas**

7   **Andes**

8   **The Pacific—Polynesia and Micronesia**

9   **Southern Africa and Madagascar**

10   **Indonesia, Philippines and Malaysia**

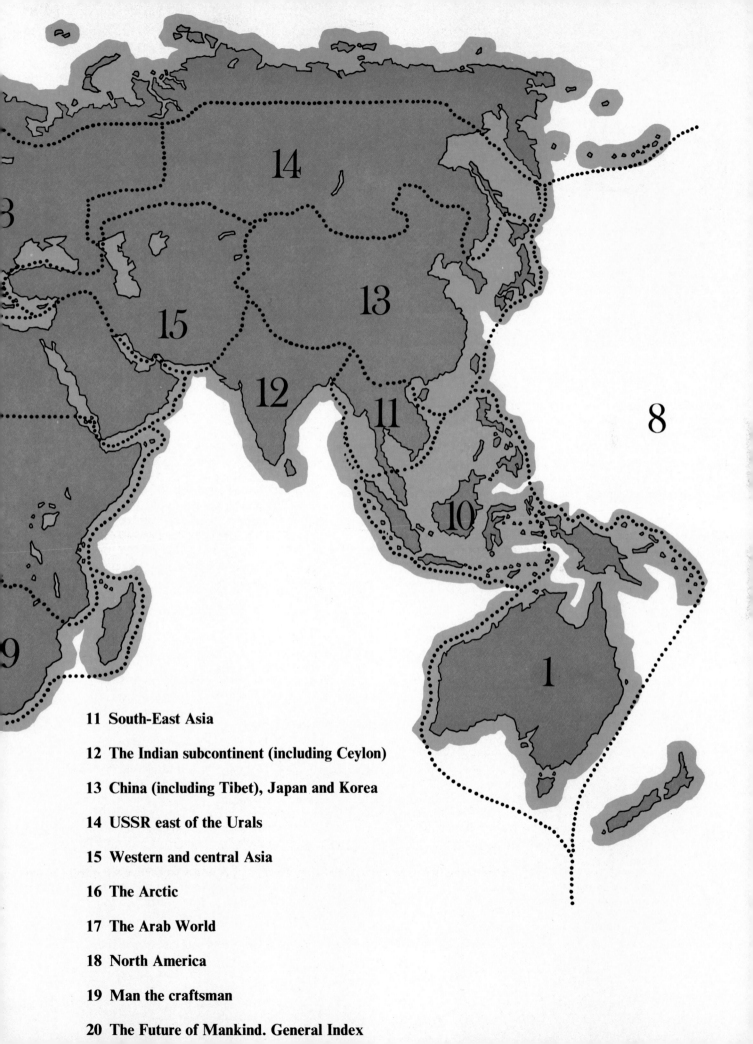

The variety of sexual patterns

In the whole range of human societies, there are just four principal forms of marital arrangement: monogamy, polygyny, polyandry and group marriage. The commonest forms of marriage are monogamy and polygyny. In monogamy husband and wife form a pair; in polygyny a husband has a plurality of wives; in polyandry a wife has a plurality of husbands. Although both polygyny and polyandry are called polygamy, which means a plurality of spouses, the term is commonly used to refer to polygyny. In group marriage, a group of men and women have reciprocal sexual rights in each other. Polyandry is comparatively rare; group marriage much rarer.

Monogamy is the accepted form of marriage in western societies which have been profoundly influenced by the Judaeo-Christian thought and tradition. Only in our own day has the validity of monogamous marriage been questioned. However, comparisons between the conception of marriage in the contemporary USA, in South America and in the Mediterranean countries makes it clear that the institution is by no means monolithic in its structure. In the USA there is great fluidity and a new recognition of the rights of the woman. In South America and the Mediterranean complete fidelity is expected of the wife, associated with freedom for the male to take a mistress.

In the United States the industrial and technological advances of the last 25 years have produced a society in which the individual may feel rejected and uncertain. These pressures lead to the questioning of the institutional framework of the society, and marriage becomes a matter of experimentation, by encounter groups for example, and in group sex. Group sex is a particularly interesting phenomenon, as it occurs mainly among middle class surburbanites. 'Swinging,' as it is called, is practised by groups of married couples, with the occasional invitation to a single individual. It may either be private, when partners are exchanged and intercourse takes place privately; or intercourse may take place publicly at a party and partners are chosen indiscriminately.

In contrast to this reinterpretation of monogamy in the USA are those societies described as Mediterranean. Far less susceptible to change, they maintain a strictly traditional attitude towards marriage. A double standard of sexual morals demands complete chastity from the wife, while the husband is permitted to indulge in extra-marital sex providing the overt structure of the family is maintained. Slower technological change and the strong influence of the Roman Catholic Church have inhibited any tendency to change the conception of marriage.

Scandinavia is another variant in the western model of monogamy. Christianity came late to these countries – in the 11th century – and the influence of the Church has been negligible in determining the relationship of the sexes. There is a tradition of equality between men and women which leads to a much greater understanding of the demands of marriage. Another factor is the very liberal attitude towards sexual experimentation by young people.

Somewhere between the rigid attitudes of the Mediterranean, and the liberal views of the USA, are the attitudes of Britain and the rest of Europe. Undoubtedly the institution of marriage in its traditional form is being questioned, but the questioning has not yet assumed the overt form of experimentation found in the USA.

The west has no monopoly of monogamy – it is the preferred form of marriage in a number of societies throughout the world. For example the Vedda, an aboriginal tribe of Ceylon, are so strictly monogamous that they have the extreme penalty of death for adultery. The Victorian notion that monogamy was the highest, most evolved form of marriage cannot be substantiated.

Polygyny, the plurality of wives, occurs in most human societies depending, obviously enough, upon the availability of women. In the majority of African states, it coexists with monogamy. To take more than one wife is a sign of prestige: generally it is only the more affluent who can afford them. Polygyny is found among relatively undeveloped peoples in many African tribal societies, as well as among the great range of Islamic societies from North Africa to Indonesia.

The European view is that polygyny inevitably connotes the subjugation of women. This is not necessarily the case, as control of such households does not always rest with the male spouse. Wives can group together to exert pressure on the husband to do what they wish in a variety of ways. The children in such families are exposed to more adult contacts than those of the monogamous unit: the result is a broader social education which is beneficial.

Polyandry, compared with both monogamy and polygyny, is comparatively rare. Two major areas where it is found are the Himalayas and South India, which provides the classical example of polyandry; the Toda of the Nilgiri Hills, described here by W H R Rivers in *The Toda*, London 1906: '... The Toda have a completely organized and definite system of polyandry. When a woman marries a man, it is understood that she becomes the wife of his brothers at the same time. When a boy is married to a girl, not only are his brothers regarded as the husbands of the girl, but any brother later born will similarly be regarded as sharing his older brother's rights ... The brothers live together, and my informants seemed to regard as a ridiculous idea that there should even be disputes or jealousies of the kind that might be expected in such a household. When the wife becomes pregnant, the eldest brother (or the co-husband) performs the ceremony of giving the bow and arrow by which the paternity of the child is established, but the brothers are all regarded equally as the father of the child.'

It has been suggested that Tibetan polyandry may be

Fernando Henriques

economic. In Tibet, land is extremely fragmented. One son of a family will go into the religious life. His brothers will marry a single wife and continue to farm the land. To afford a wife of one's own indicates an improved economic position. In Tibetan society three of the four major forms of marriage coexist.

Although apparently alien to European tradition, polyandry is not entirely unknown in the west. Both Polybius in his *Historia*, XIII, and Xenephon in *Lacemoniorum Republica*, 9 indicate that fraternal polyandry existed in ancient Sparta. More recently, in periods of economic depression in both Europe and the United States, polyandrous households have developed. The co-husband in such cases is known, euphemistically, as the lodger.

Group marriage is so rare that some have doubted whether it exists at all. However, there is no question of the authenticity of this type of marriage, formerly current in the Marquesa Islands in the Pacific, which Ralph Linton has described in *The Individual and his Society*. '. . . The household consisted of the main husband, the wife or wives, and a series of subsidiary husbands . . . In theory all members of the household had sexual rights, even servants had access to the head wife if they so wished; actually the first husband ran things and distributed favors, although it was to his advantage to see that his underlings were sexually satisfied, so that they would work for his house and not wander off with other women . . .'

Whatever the marital arrangements preferred in society, there are always prohibitions as to whom one may marry. The taboo extends from close biological kin to those with no blood relationship, but who are classified socially as kinsfolk. Western societies have also had most taboos with no biological justification, such as a widower being forbidden to marry his wife's sister. The most universal of prohibitions are those concerned with close blood relatives: brother and sister, father and daughter, mother and son.

Older theories of incest suggested that there is an inherent antagonism against intercourse between kinsfolk. Research, however, has shown on the contrary that there may be strong sexual attraction between the members of a family group, which is inhibited by the incest taboos. Brenda Seligman describes the function of the taboos in her essay *The Problem of Incest and Exogamy* (American Anthropologist July-September 1950). 'The survival value of the incest prohibitions has been so important that it has become a universal law, the basis of both moral law and of social organization. The incest prohibitions lessen the grave source of friction which may arise from the maintenance of adolescents within the family group, due to sexual jealousy and competition between father and son for the possession of females of the two generations. The adolescents, freed from this anxiety by means of the accepted taboo, can assist in obtaining the food supply and in protecting the group. Thus, the family, instead of being an animal protective group, becomes a human protective one . . .'

Despite the general horror with which incest is regarded, prohibitions are frequently broken, and the offense tolerated. B Malinowsky in *Crime and Custom in Savage Society* (London 1932), writes that '. . . in the Trobriand Islands I found that the breach of exogamy – as regards intercourse and not marriage – is by no means a rare occurence, and public opinion is lenient, though decidedly hypocritical. If the affair is carried on *sub rosa* with a certain amount of decorum, and if no one in particular stirs up trouble, public opinion will gossip but not demand any harsh punishment. If, on the contrary, scandal breaks out – everyone turns against the guilty pair and by ostracism and insults one or the other may be driven to suicide . . .'

The one barrier which must never be flouted, and this is true for all societies, is that of mother-son incest, although there are paradoxical situations by which prohibitions, binding on the mass of the people, might be flouted by the royal family or clan. In some instances they were even enjoined to do so: among the Inca, in Hawaii, Ancient Egypt and among the Azande of the Eastern Sudan. The Avungara, the royal clan of the Azande, openly encourage both father-daughter and brother-sister sexual relationships. It is possible that in all these cases license to break the taboo is connected with the magical powers of kingship.

There are magical connotations too in the sanction sometimes given for an individual to have incestuous relations in order to invest himself with exceptional powers. Among the Thonga of South Africa, a hippopotamus hunter will, on occasion, have intercourse with his daughter to give him power over his prey. 'This incestuous act, which is strongly taboo in ordinary life, has made him into a "murderer": he has killed something at home; he has acquired the courage necessary for doing great deeds on the river' (H Junod *The life of a South African tribe*).

Incest taboos are universal whatever their explanation; their very existence indicates a basic sexual attraction between near kin. These taboos restrict sexual intercourse and the choice of a mate. But there are other barriers which inhibit sexual expression. In their attitudes towards pre-marital sexual activity, societies range from very restrictive to very permissive.

Traditionally, western society comes into the smallest, though geographically extensive, restrictive category. Societies that are restrictive in their approach to pre-marital sexual activity range from North America to the East Indies. The Ashanti forbid their boys to masturbate or indulge in any sexual play; Kwoma boys of New Guinea are beaten on the penis by a woman if they are seen with an erection; Cuna Indian children of Panama are given no sex instruction until they are literally on the 9 point of marriage. Sexual activity in the young is most effectively restricted as in our western society – by keeping the sexes apart. Societies most successful at this appear to be from the Americas, for example, the Arapaho, Cheyenne and Papago. The Wapisians of Guyana discovered a most ingenious way round the problem of pre-marital sex; cohabitation was equated with marriage so that by one single act of intercourse a marriage was established.

But however successful the supervision, there were bound to be breaches of these rules. In small groups, separation of the sexes may have successfully kept sexual activity among the young to a minimum, but in large, complex societies the problem is greater. The ideal norm – the chaste bride and the groom who had sown a few wild oats – of northern European peasant societies, seems to have been typical only of middle and upper classes: among the mass of the people a different picture emerges. A number of courting customs runs counter to this ideal norm. Known as 'night running' in Norway, 'night courting' in Sweden, 'proving night' in Germany and in Britain as 'running in the night,' they involve sexual play, and in most cases intercourse.

In the German *probenächte,* for example, the young suitor had to make his way to his girl through her bedroom window. For the first few visits both remained clad and sat and talked. But, after a time, decorum disappeared. 'In due course, the girl gives her lover, amid all sorts of bucolic jesting and teasing, an opportunity to get acquainted with her secret charms; she lets him surprise her lightly clothed, and, at last, grants him everything with which a woman can gratify the sensuality of a man. Yet even then a certain gradation is observed. Very often the girl refuses to grant her lover his final wish until he uses force. This always happens when there is some doubt of his physical strength.' (F C Fisher *Über die Probenächte der Deutschen Bauermädchen*).

There seems to be a definite connection between such customs and the 'trial marriage' which has a long history in Europe. The Swedish sociologist, Alva Myrdal, suggests that this could only take place in small, tightly controlled communities, where everyone knew each other. The trial marriage discouraged promiscuity and marriage followed upon pregnancy.

Somewhere between the restrictive and the permissive groups are those semi-restrictive societies in the Americas, in many parts of New Guinea which profess strict control of adolescent sexual activity but do little to punish it. Though parents in Alorese society in Indonesia disapprove of the sexual play of young people, the young continue to imitate the sexual roles of their elders undeterred, unless their behavior is blatant.

Sexually permissive societies are by far the most numerous and widespread. In these, attitudes range from open tolerance to active encouragement of youthful sexual exploits. The Valave of Madagascar encourage

sexual play even in very young children; parents take pleasure in watching and applauding their behavior. This is also true of the Nandi and other Central African peoples. On the other hand, the practice of clitoridectomy – or 'female circumcision' – is widely practiced as an initiation rite among various peoples, particularly in Africa and the Arab world, the purpose apparently being to diminish the women's sexual pleasure and so to encourage rectitude. (Male circumcision, widely practised throughout the world at various ages between infancy and puberty, probably has its origins in hygiene.)

Sexual tolerance for the young is sometimes institutionalized, as in a number of societies in New Guinea, India, Melanesia, the Philippines and Africa. Here in the village dormitory – a sort of residential youth club – young people of both sexes manage their own affairs. The most highly developed form is the *ghotul* of the Muria of Bastar State in India. Adults have no authority in the *ghotul* and adolescents form their own society within the larger group, electing two leaders of their own.

More typical is the Trobriand *bukumatula*. The Trobrianders are totally uninhibited about youthful sexuality but '... it is obvious that the lasting liaisons of youths and adult girls require some special institution, more definitely established, more physically comfortable, and at the same time having the approval of custom. To meet this need, tribal custom and etiquette offer accommodation and privacy in the form of the *bukumatula*, the bachelors' and unmarried girls' house . . . In this a limited number of couples, some two, three, or four, live for longer or shorter periods together in a temporary community...' (B Malinowsky *The sexual life of savages*).

But the *bukumatula* does not encourage unrestrained promiscuity. To attempt intercourse with a girl other than your own is as disgraceful as adultery with a friend's wife. The *bukumatula* exists for pure enjoyment, based on mutual sexual attraction. Liaisons begun in the *bukumatula* may not always result in marriage.

The Trobriand solution to a problem which confronts all societies seems remarkably sane and logical. Restrictive societies demand impossibly high standards of sexual behavior from their young at a time when they are at their sexual peak. Such repression might have long-term deleterious effects, or lead to deceit and clandestine activity. Until quite recently in western society widespread prostitution was a common result.

There are important variations in societies all over the world in coitus itself, both in the act of intercourse and the restrictions placed upon it. The most usual position for coitus in western society is where the female lies down with the man above her. The reasons may be found in early Christian view of marriage and sex: the doctrine that marriage is exclusively for the perpetuation of the human race, and chastity infinitely to be preferred. St Thomas Aquinas' view was that although marriage was not contrary to the love of God it was nevertheless an obstacle to it. There was no notion of pleasure in sex; 'to have intercourse except for procreation is to do injury to nature' (Clement of Alexandria *Paedogosus*). This philosophy ordained how intercourse should take place. In the Middle Ages, theologians debated whether any variation from the 'normal' position was a mortal or a venial sin. Aquinas was inclined to think it was mortal, whereas Sanchez considered it merely venial. Their reasons varied from the possibility that other positions might enhance sexual pleasure and detract from the business in hand – procreation – to the possibility that if the man were supine there was less chance of conception. Attenuated as these beliefs may be today, they are sufficiently strong for Kinsey in his *Sexual behavior in the human male* to state that a considerable number in his sample thought that the reversal of the 'normal' position was essentially a perversion.

The Church was not only concerned with the coital position but also with the frequency of intercourse. In the medieval period it was forbidden on Sundays, feast days and fast days. It was left to the sinner as to whether he should indulge himself during Lent and Advent. Abstinence was obligatory before taking Communion.

Pre-Christian Europe had no such inhibitions. Witness Ovid in his *Art of Love*: 'Let each woman know herself; from your own bodies fix your methods; one fashion does not suit all alike. Let her who is fair of face recline upon her back; let those whose backs please them be seen from behind. . . . A small woman should ride astride . . . There are a thousand modes of love.'

Some non-European civilizations were also pre-occupied with frequency of intercourse. The *Laws of Manu* laid down that for Hindus, two weeks in each month were to be allowed as days of sexual pleasure. The Talmud is more specific: frequency varied according to occupation. The scholar was permitted to have intercourse once a week, the laborer twice a week, and the youth without occupation once a day.

Regulation apart, these societies produced a number of texts which convey in great detail everything which concerns the art of love. In the years since World War II, new editions of works such as the *Kama Sutra* and *Ananga-Ranga* have appeared: there is no equivalent of these erotic treatises in the west.

In pre-literate societies, there is a far greater variety of coital positions than in western societies. In societies in Polynesia, Indonesia and East and Central Africa, the positions which appear to be dominant are variants of the face-to-face posture. In others such as the Masai, Kwakuitl of the north-west coast of America and some South American Indians the favored position is for the couple to lie on their sides facing each other. Circumstance will often dictate the position adopted; where the couple fear detection, coitus takes place in a standing position and the man enters from behind: in a crowded hut the method used is the one least likely to disturb.

Amid the great variations of sexual behavior in human societies, there is one constant which affects all – menstruation. To the man this is the most mysterious aspect of woman: in all societies blood is held to be sacred or divine.

Most human societies prohibit sexual intercourse during menstruation. Women are not only regarded as unclean at this time but as positively maleficent. To neutralize the evil supposed to emanate from them, they are sometimes secluded in a special place. The menstruous woman is regarded with awe. Some Australian aboriginal groups believe that copulation with a woman who is menstruating will cause their bodies to degenerate; other groups in the Pacific are firmly of the opinion that it induces blindness. Coition is not the only way that evil is passed on to men. Many African societies believe that touching a garment or food of a woman in menstruation is sufficient to bring disaster – illness or the loss of his virility to the male.

There are rare instances where the menstrual taboo is reversed. Among some groups of Maoris, the Walapai Indians of Arizona on the island of Truk in the Pacific and among the A-Kamba of East Africa intercourse is not only permitted during menstruations, but positively enjoined. Among the A-Kamba, described by C W Hobley in *Ethnology of the Akamba and other East African Tribes*, '. . . when a married woman menstruates, the husband cohabits with her that night, the idea being that she will probably conceive . . .'

While there are no positive injunctions in western societies against coition during the woman's monthly period, there is nevertheless a considerable folklore associated with the dangers of the menstruous woman, which may well be based on the powerful Semitic exhortations. 'If a man copulateth with her in the time of her flowers, he shall be unclean seven days: and every bed on which he shall sleep shall be defiled' (*Leviticus* XV, 24). In a similar way the ancient Hindu *Laws of Manu* state: '. . . the wisdom, the energy, the strength, the right, and the vitality of a man who approaches a woman covered with menstrual excrement, utterly perish.' The Christian church's opinion of this has varied over the centuries. In earlier periods intercourse during menstruation was utterly condemned: later theologians such as Sanchez and Liguori were prepared to permit it. R Biffault, in his book *The Mothers*, shows that folklore on the other hand has been fairly consistent in associating the menstruous woman with untoward effects on both human, vegetable and animal substances. The woman will sour wine, ruin the making of butter and harm the manufacture of sugar. It was a view supported by medical opinion in England as late as the 19th century. In the *British Medical Journal* (Vol I 1878) it was stated that there was absolutely no doubt that if a menstruating woman attempted to cure a ham, the operation would be unsuccessful.

11

Peoples of highland South Americ

In 1532, a handful of Spaniards led by Francisco Pizarro captured, as a going concern, a whole empire in a few weeks. Although a further forty years passed before all opposition faded, the fall of the Inca Empire must rank as one of the most spectacular conquests in history. When the Spaniards arrived on the west coast of South America the Inca Empire had reached its greatest territorial expansion but there were already signs that it would expand no further. The dynastic dispute at the time of Pizarro's landing indicated that all was not well in Tahuantinsuyu – the realm of the four quarters – and that the Empire had outgrown the capacities of its system of central control.

The Inca Empire is well known because of the historical documents describing its nature and conquest, but that empire was not the only advanced civilization of the Andean coast. It was simply the most recent, and probably the most successful, in a succession of such civilizations about which we lack historical documents but know a great deal – for two reasons. One is the environment in which these civilizations flourished. As the climate, especially along stretches of coast from north Peru southward, is very dry, many objects which would have decayed under more humid conditions have been found in a wonderful state of preservation. Tapestry, cloth, maize seed, and even human corpses have survived more or less intact until the present day. Secondly, members of these civilizations were great potters and constructors of huge stone cities and buildings, many of which – like Tiahuanaco in Bolivia – stand today relatively unharmed by the passage of time. Archaeologists have been able to learn a great deal about the prehistory of some of the more important areas, and although there are still gaps in our knowledge, they can demonstrate in many places a sequence of cultures reaching back over 5,000 years. Perhaps one of the most exciting of recent suggestions is that an important factor in the culture development of the area was the arrival around 3,000 BC in Ecuador of colonizers from Japan.

On both sides of the area the Andes rise sharply: on the west from a fairly narrow coastal plain, and to the east from the Amazonian basin. The steep mountain slopes are in striking contrast with the flatness of the eastern lowlands of South America and account for rapid changes in environment and economy. The Peruvian town of Pucallpa, for example, stands at just 500 feet above sea-level at the foot of the Andes on the Ucayali river, 2,800 miles from the mouth of the Amazon of which it is a tributary. To the west, in much less than quarter the distance, there are mountain peaks that reach to 18,000 feet. These differences have been accentuated by the way the Andean slopes are divided into numerous small valleys separated by sharp mountain spurs. The Andean range is not so much a single cordillera as a number of parallel chains of mountains interspersed with valleys and plateaux – of which the most famous is the Altiplano of the central Andes where the great lake of Titicaca lies. The typical Andean valley suffers from seasonal water shortages and has such steep sides and so narrow a flat bottom that little of the land is suitable for agriculture, except by extensive hillside terracing and irrigation. The shortage of good land and the fact that productive zones are next-door to unproductive zones may well have influenced the development of warfare and trade – two characteristic features of the region.

In the markets of the Andes the different regions exchange their products. The communication system of the Inca Empire at the time of conquest stretched from the Colombian frontier in the north to approximately where Santiago, capital of Chile, stands today. Like the communication system of the Roman Empire, which it equalled, it was primarily strategic in purpose, but also had great economic importance. Perhaps the most famous example of this is the transport of fresh fish from the coast to the highlands by relays of runners.

Though the nature of the terrain often encouraged contact between different peoples, not infrequently it resulted in the opposite. The isolation of some mountain valleys has meant that even today there are Quechuan and Aymaran communities whose ways of thought and life have changed little since the Europeans arrived. Where some peoples have been left aside by the events of the last four hundred years, others have made conscious efforts to avoid them. For example, the Kogi of northern Colombia have retreated further and further into the uplands of the Sierra Nevada de Santa Marta.

The arrival of the Spaniards had rapid and startling results, mainly of a demographic nature. There was a very sharp drop in the population and most of it can be attributed to the effect of imported infectious diseases. The population was also considerably dispersed and redistributed. Some migrated voluntarily to escape from their new rulers, but for many the migration was compulsory. The Spaniards had taken over a traditional system of slave labor known as *mita* and adapted it to their own ends and needs – largely the provision of a labor force to work in the silver mines. Today the modern counterparts of those silver mines are the Bolivian tin mines; although they are no longer drafted to the mines, the miners are an important and dissident element in the national politics of Bolivia.

Although the search for gold and for converts were the driving forces behind the Spanish conquest, it was not only precious metals they transported to Europe from their new colonies. Many items we now regard as everyday objects originated in the New World. The potato – which has become a central part of our diet – was the staple food of many Highland Indians, who had developed for its storage an effective means of freeze-drying. The potatoes, exposed alternately to frost and sun, were reduced to a dehydrated mass called *chuñu*.

Peanuts, cocaine, and quinine also come from here, as does the guinea pig which was (and is) kept as a domestic animal and eaten. A recent and curious borrowing by the Old World from the New has been the technique of reed boat construction. Thor Heyerdahl, after the failure of his first attempt to cross the Atlantic in his African built papyrus raft, Ra I, turned to the Aymaran boat builders of Lake Titicaca who constructed the successful Ra II.

The flow of cultural loans was by no means entirely one-way and, among the items which the Spaniards brought with them, the horse must rank as one of the most important. In the high Andes the llama was the indigenous beast of burden, and although it can only carry small loads it has never been superseded at the higher altitudes. Elsewhere, man was the beast of burden and the advent of the horse had fascinating results. To a degree the horse was instrumental in the Spaniards' rapid success in overthrowing the Inca empire; but where Indians adopted the horse, they turned it with great effect against its introducer. The Guajiro Indians – who live at the northern end of the continent on Guajiro peninsula – adopted both horses and cattle from the Europeans. As early as the mid-16th century they had developed a successful nomadic economy which has survived until today – partly, no doubt, due to the inhospitable nature of their territory which has deterred other settlers. The Araucanian Indians of southern Chile, at the other end of the continent, who had proved an insurmountable obstacle to the further southward expansion of Inca territory, presented an equally difficult task both for the Spaniards and their Chilean successors. The Araucanians incorporated horses in a highly effective form of guerilla warfare which, coupled with a warrantedly deceitful diplomacy, allowed them to keep their freedom until the last quarter of the 19th century. The descendants of those Indians, the Mapuche, now live on reservations, or drift into the cities, and face all the problems of land shortages and detribalization.

Although the Guajiro at the northern extreme of South America managed to adapt and survive, this is far from true of the indigenous peoples who populated the southern extremity of the continent. The Chono, Alacaluf and Yahgan tribes, collectively often known as the Canoe Indians, have virtually disappeared without trace. The land they inhabited is the wet, cold coastline of Tierra del Fuego and northwards; their technology was one of the poorest known to man – equalled perhaps only by the Tasmanians'. Their dress, their diet, and their shelters all seem totally ill-adapted to the rigors of the climate. One of these Indians, known as Jeremy Button, became ephemerally famous when he was brought back to London in the 1830's by the surveying ship *Beagle* (on which Darwin had sailed), but otherwise they have passed into oblivion.

The Foot Indians, in contrast to the Canoe Indians, lived inland, and knew nothing of navigation. The poorest and most southerly of these were the Ona who lived in the interior of Tierra del Fuego, while on the mainland of Patagonia were to be found the Tehuelche and to the north of them the Puelche. The economy of all these peoples was based on hunting the guanaco (the wild form of the llama) and the rhea (the South American ostrich). All these peoples except the Ona quickly saw the advantages the horse offered their way of life, and they took to hunting the guanaco and the rhea from horseback using the weapon known as the *bolas*. The *bolas* is similar to the lasso, but in place of a noose the rope divides into three strands with a heavy ball weight secured to the end of each. However, the fate of these Indians was the same as that of the Plains Indians of North America; they quickly disappeared as the advancing Argentinian cattle herders and sheep farmers took over their land. Among those people who today inhabit the plains of Patagonia, where the Indians once hunted, perhaps the most unusual are the communities of Welsh-speaking sheep farmers, who arrived there during the last century.

Spanish is everywhere the common national language of all the countries, but there are both rural and urban communities who speak the language of their forefathers. As well as the large numbers of Europeans other than those of Spanish extraction – there is a fascinating intermixture of Spanish and Irish names in Chile – there is also an African element in the population. There was less need for African slaves along the west coast of South America than in Brazil, and accordingly the negroid element is smaller and mainly confined to the lowlands from Ecuador northwards. In many areas the Amerindian population still dominates: Quechuan, the language of the Incas, is, after Spanish, the most widespread – as it was when the Spaniards arrived. The bulk of the Indian population is to be found in the Highlands, mainly in Peru, and also in Bolivia and Ecuador, which have a very high proportion of Amerindians. In the lowland areas most indigenous populations have suffered badly from European intrusion, and tribes such as the Cayapa have managed to survive only because their territories are unsuitable for non-Amerindian settlement.

Most European descendants live in the cities. Just as the preconquest civilizations were largely urban, so the Spaniards brought with them a mainly urban culture. The cities which they built contain many masterpieces of colonial architecture; and there is no drab uniformity about the towns and cities of the region. Each city has its own peculiar character; there is La Paz at 12,000 feet above sea-level, Quito often referred to as the City of Eternal Spring, and Lima, the City of Kings. But of all of them it is perhaps Cuzco which enshrines the whole history of the area. Once the royal city of the Incas, its massive stones and foundations now form a Spanish colonial and modern Peruvian city thronged with Amerindians, *mestizos* and tourists.

Guajiro
Colombia

The Guajiro who live on the largely desert peninsula of La Guajira on the Colombia-Venezuela border have a special talent for survival. It was here that they escaped over four hundred years ago from Spanish pursuit and conquest which wiped out about 96 per cent of the indigenous population in the southern half of the continent alone. Here in the northern part of the continent, where they stood in the way of the conquistadors' thrust to the fabled gold-lands of the interior, the indigenous inhabitants suffered most – by the sword and by the epidemics which spread among them like wild-fire in the Spaniards' wake. In many parts of the northern

14

15

The Guajiro guard their
independence as nomadic cattle
herdsmen by seasonally digging
salt here at Manaure and
selling it.

Guajiro Colombia

Since the Conquest the hot,
desert Guajira peninsula has
been a refuge for the Guajiro,
here returning from a day's work
on the saltpan.

The face of this Guajiro woman
carrying a 130lb sack of salt
is blackened with charcoal and
goat's fat to protect it from
the sun.

A woman dumps her sack of salt
on a levee. The Guajiro also
mine gypsum — produced by the
evaporation of a former inland
sea.

After two months' digging salt
these men will return to their
basic occupation: wandering
over the peninsula
with their prized cattle.

coast the indigenous population swiftly disappeared. Not
however, the Guajiro. Where other Amerindian tribes
were so fragile that they collapsed in the face of the
onslaught, the Guajiro not only survived. They
prospered.

The Guajiro prosper still. Further contacts with
Europeans have failed either to subdue or submerge
them. There are 50,000 Guajiro today, the largest tribal
group in either Colombia or Venezuela and one of the
largest in all South America and they are forever alive
to new means to further their survival.

Before the Spanish drove them into their arid penin-
sular retreat the Guajiro probably lived by hunting
animals and gathering plants in the interior and shellfish
by the seashore.

But on the La Guajira peninsula then as now animal
and plant life are sparse. For most of the year the peninsula is barren and desolate, the temperature is hot
(averaging over 80°F) and the desert blooms only briefly
– between late September and November when the rain
falls in a few short, sharp downpours. In that short rainy
season the thirsty desert turns rapidly and sufficiently
green to provide good grazing for cattle, sheep and goats.
The Guajiro owe their early and continued survival in
this arid region to their adaptability: from hunting and
gathering they responded to the demands of their new
habitat and became what they are today, predominantly
herdsmen with a vigorous supporting industry in salt
and gypsum mining.

Guajiro women and girls still gather wild vegetables
and fruits, but less as a basis of their diets as last-ditch
reserves, to be resorted to in times of scarcity or famine.
They make a porridge, for example, of *enea* root by
peeling, dicing, sun-drying, grating, leeching and finally
boiling it over a low fire for about three hours. The *enea*
porridge has to be eaten the same day as by the next day
it will have turned acidic. They also eat the fruit of
various cacti: the *cardon*, *breva*, *tuna* and *buche*. But
after long disuse the Guajiro's once extensive knowledge
of preparing wild food has largely been lost.

Although game was never prolific on the peninsula
and it is now diminishing even more, the Guajiro also
still sometimes hunt, with guns and traps. With dogs
they hunt the small red deer that frequent the hills round
Nazret. They hunt rabbits with dogs, rifle and bow and
arrow – which they also use to shoot doves, partridges,
duck and other smaller birds. They fish with hooks and
nets along the lagoons and coastlines, sometimes catching
lobster, molluscs and crabs.

The Guajiro became the skilled, successful nomadic
cattle herdsmen they are today in response to the
Spaniard's stimulus over 400 years ago just as today
they respond to the arrival of industrialization. By
selling their labor, they buy their continued independence.
The Guajiro know the value of money. Today they sell
their labor in the oil-producing area of Lake Maracaibo. 17

(Over page) From the salt pan at
Manaure the money-conscious
Guajiro transport and sell salt
far afield in Colombia and
Venezuela.

Guajiro Colombia

14-year-old Rita Gueron whose roving parents have gone off to guard the lighthouse at Punta Gallinas finds solace with her pet rabbit.

Or the Guajiro from Colombia cross the border to Venezuela to find work building roads: Venezuelan money, they claim, is of greater value than Colombian pesos.

On the north-west coast of the peninsula the Guajiro work their own mines, extracting light minerals: gypsum, produced by the evaporation of a former inland sea, which lies packed between layers of white clay under the sand, the Guajiro export from the port of Portere; and salt they dig at Manaure, then transport over, and beyond, the peninsula. The miners tend to exploit the deposits for just two months of the year, leaving the rest of the year free for the real business of this people, cattle.

When the Spaniards arrived the Guajiro controlled rich pearl beds, a more lasting source of wealth than gold which can easily be looted, and one which the Guajiro had the secret of exploiting. The Spaniards too were conscious of the attractions and advantages of pearls and were prepared to trade first sheep and goats, then pigs and chickens and finally horses, donkeys and cattle if the Guajiro would, in exchange, gather and trade the precious pearls for them. Then too the Guajiro saw the potential of trading their labor. They were to be rewarded. They quickly learned how to herd first goats, then cattle from the Spaniards, who were expert herdsmen. By 1550 cattle were abundant on the peninsula. By adopting pastoralism the Guajiro made themselves unique in the New World. By doing it so well they grew rich and numerous. Meat and milk, instead of wild plants and animals, became the basis of their diet; and cattle-owning the basis not only of their livelihood, but of the entire structure of their society.

Water is short all year round, except in the short September-November rainy season when rainfall is so abundant that roads on the peninsula become impassable. The coastal regions especially suffer from drought. Here the coastal Guajiro have made ingenious wells, called *jaguey*, about nine feet deep and encircled by wood from the cardon cactus to collect and retain the water for as long as possible. The water rarely lasts the whole of the dry season and the governments of both Colombia and Venezuela are exploring ways to help with excavated wells and reservoirs. The lives of the Guajiro cattle herdsmen are necessarily nomadic.

Men and boys – wearing possibly a wide-brimmed straw hat, possibly a shirt or jacket, but invariably a short loincloth tied round the waist with a tasselled string or belt holding a knitted string bag or knife, and a sash to carry their arrows – can be seen wandering all over the peninsula grazing and watering their herds. It is the woman's role in the Guajiro cattle industry to prepare the meat from the beasts, milk the cows and make the cheese.

The women wear hats, of which they are proud, tied over their long hair with bright cotton kerchiefs, with which they also protect their faces from the hot sun and

the sand whipped up by the wind. But a Guajiro woman's proudest possession is often her necklace – pale reddish *tuma* stones interspersed with gold beads and ending with gold animals like turtles and frogs – which she wears over her *manta*, a large tunic dress which reaches to the ground. These necklaces are priceless, highly prized and passed down from mother to daughter. Guajiro men and women alike wear leather sandals, the women's decorated with big colored pom-poms, to protect their feet from the burning sand. Guajiro women paint their faces and other parts of their skin with yellow, brown and black powder, made from a mixture of goats' fat, charcoal and a variety of bark or fungus, and often applied in complex patterns. It is said to protect the skin from the sun and desert sands.

When the women are not caring for the cattle they work at a number of skilled crafts. They spin and weave with wild cotton and occasionally wool. They make beautiful long-lasting hammocks, bright belts for the men, and large variety of sashes and bags, and they weave mats with *enea* reed. They also make pots with long coils of clay.

Since the Guajiro spend much of their time moving with their cattle, their houses are not elaborate. When actually on the move they are content with only a simple windbreak. A more permanent house is made with walls of wattle-and-daub and a gabled roof, thatched with *sara* palm leaves, *enea* reeds or split cactus. As the Guajiro acquire wealth through cattle, they build brick and cement houses. A permanent village a *rancheria* with 200 to 250 people, has 50 or so houses set apart at gunshot distance to prevent surprise attacks, and is surrounded with a cactus hedge.

The entire structure of Guajiro family and social life revolves around and is even defined by cattle. They live in some 30 matrilineal family groups called *castas* each with its own territory and identified with a particular animal. The *casta*, a Spanish name which covers an extended family of many kinsfolk, is so fundamentally linked with its cattle that one cannot exist without the other. The senior mother's brother is considered as the chief of the *casta*. His prestige, based on his own, his family's and his *casta's* accumulated wealth, is a matter of great importance to him and the members of his group. The individual's life-cycle, and his values, are bound up with his *casta*. The *casta* must do everything to protect each of its members, and the individual must reciprocate by doing everything to defend it.

Above all each member must protect the *casta's* property – its cattle. What increases the wealth of the *casta* is good: what decreases it is criminal. Theft of cattle is punished as severely as is the violation of a woman. In both cases it is the honor of the *casta* which has been abused. When a couple marry the bride price is paid in cattle: if no cattle are given the children of the marriage are hardly considered legitimate. Indeed it is

21

Guajiro Colombia

Great sea turtles are laid on their backs to stop them escaping. The Guajiro fish along the coast with hooks and nets catching shellfish.

said that in the past, wives who were not paid for in cattle were expelled from the *casta*. As one Guajiro remarked: 'I was very pleased when I had a boy child. I considered him to be a little horse, and I regarded my daughter as if she was a little cow, since cows are the greatest wealth we possess.'

The Guajiro recognize two kinds of relatives: those on the father's side, called 'blood relatives' and those on the mother's side, who are called 'flesh relatives.' In the *casta* it is the 'flesh relatives' who are the more important. The senior mother's brother, as head of the *casta* is responsible for the well-being of every member of his *casta*. Although girls must marry husbands from another *casta* of comparable wealth and status, the matrilineal kinsman will watch over a pregnant relative with the greatest care to ensure that the right taboos are observed during the pregnancy. The expectant mother will go to her mother or another member of her *casta* when her child is due. Only her matrilineal relatives may be present at the birth and they are responsible if anything goes wrong. If she should die during the birth the matrilineal relatives will be blamed and will have to return the bridewealth to the widower. Abortion is a crime against

A Guajiro trims goat meat for cooking. Meat and milk products have been their staple diet since they learnt to be skilled herdsmen 400 years ago.

(Top) Keen intelligence, hardihood and tribal solidarity have meant survival for this Guajiro – one of the most populous S. American tribes.

(Center) A donkey lugs water jars through the cacti. Only 2 months' rainfall means scarce water. It is stored in special wells – *jaguey*.

the whole *casta*.

After the birth many gifts are presented and there is much celebration in which the *casta* rather than the child's father is more involved. The mother will name her child after an ancestor or a living member of her *casta*, and the child will also have a *casta* name, rather like a surname. He will also be given a third name, a nick-name, used by all except his closest relatives.

From birth and until after he has been weaned, the child's closest relationship is with his mother. Then the mother becomes more formal and strict to teach the child to behave correctly. His father's attitude too becomes increasingly reserved, and he takes less and less part in his education and discipline. As the child grows up he develops a close relationship instead with his grandparents and maternal uncles who take special care to see that he is correctly taught. From the age of about nine a child grows closer to his uncle, and may even go to live in his house and tend his cattle. A daughter's early education too will be looked after by her mother, but as she grows up and draws near to marriage she becomes the responsibility of her aunt. And it is members of her aunt's *casta* who see that the ceremonies at puberty are correctly managed.

It is the mother's brother, as in other matrilineal societies, who tends to dominate a young person's life. He acts not only as his adviser but also as his ultimate legal representative. If a young man commits the grave Guajiro crime of killing a cow for example, its angry owner will seek compensation not from his father, but from his uncle who is responsible for the debt. Where the offense is so serious that the boy's life is demanded in recompense, the boy can rely on his uncle to protect him. The affair may start a vendetta between two *castas* that can last for generations since the life of any other member of the *casta* can be taken in recompense instead. A nephew inherits his maternal uncle's property, cattle and position when he dies. Girls also seek advice from their maternal uncles, except in specifically feminine matters when they consult instead their maternal aunt or grandmother.

The people of a *casta* and its cattle are treated as practically identical: cattle, like people, are taken to a shaman if they are sick. A woman who eats her own cattle commits incest – for she is then mixing the flesh, which, like marrying a member of one's own *casta*, is forbidden. Cattle sacrificed at a funeral must not be eaten by the relatives of the dead man, as this would be tantamount to eating his flesh.

When a Guajiro dies his *casta* is responsible for the proper preparation of his corpse, for his funeral, and for sending him off properly on the long journey of his spirit existence. The total number of cattle slaughtered to feed the guests from other *castas* at the funeral is remembered and credited to the spirit *casta*. For even beyond the grave the *casta* and its cattle are one.

Cities of highland South America

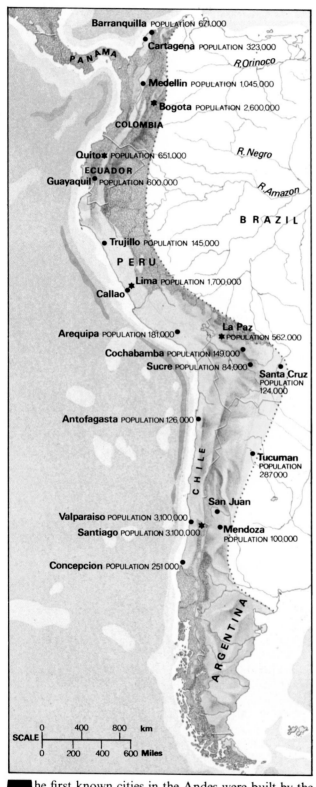

Barranquilla POPULATION 671,000

Cartagena POPULATION 323,000

PANAMA

R.Orinoco

● Medellin POPULATION 1,045,000

✱ Bogota POPULATION 2,600,000

COLOMBIA

R. Negro

Quito✱ POPULATION 651,000

ECUADOR

Guayaquil● POPULATION 600,000

R.Amazon

B R A Z I L

● Trujillo POPULATION 145,000

P E R U

Lima POPULATION 1,700,000

Callao●✱

Arequipa POPULATION 181,000 ●

La Paz ✱POPULATION 562,000

Cochabamba POPULATION 149,000 ●

Sucre POPULATION 84,000 ●

Santa Cruz POPULATION 124,000 ●

Antofagasta POPULATION 126,000 ●

Tucuman POPULATION 287000 ●

C H I L E

San Juan

Valparaiso POPULATION 3,100,000

Santiago POPULATION 3,100,000 ✱

● Mendoza POPULATION 100,000

A R G E N T I N A

Concepcion POPULATION 251 000 ●

SCALE
0   400   800   km
0 200 400 600 Miles

The first known cities in the Andes were built by the Incas, long before the Spaniards came, when the legendary Children of the Sun came from Lake

24

25

Contrasts between poor and rich are less vivid in Chile than in neighboring states. Santiaguinos' enthusiasm for Marxist rule soon waned.

Titicaca on the Altiplano, conquered the Aymara Indians and settled in the Peruvian highlands in the 12th century. Successors to other little-known pre-Colombian civilizations, they established magnificent fortresses in the area like Machu Picchu and, overlooking Cuzco, Sacasahuaman, a gigantic complex built, like other Inca strongholds, with chiseled stone boulders fitted together so subtly and as snug as to be proof against the ever present threat of *huaicos* – earth tremors. The seaward run of the Andes lies along one of the earth's great subterranean flaws.

The approach to the city of Cuzco is memorable. You pass through gorges and the roads are twisty. Suddenly you are looking down on a flurry of pink, cupped hazily in a green basin. The initial blur of a mass of pink-tiled rectangular roofs begins to contrast with their sharp, angular shape. When the morning mists dissolve and the sun climbs high, everything is bright and clear in the rarefied air at nearly 12,000 feet above sea level.

The city is bizarre and beautiful. The architecture is a mixture of Inca and Spanish-colonial, yet the ancient Inca stone is vaster, more solid, and seems even newer, than the Spanish colonial baroque. Huge boulders provide the base of many buildings, hoisted sometimes twenty feet into position by a method no longer precisely known, irregular yet ingeniously shaped by patient human artifice to fit perfectly without mortar in a complex three-dimensional jigsaw. Often the top half is merely of adobe, simple and recently patted together. The elaborate ornament of the Spanish buildings, accentuates the overwhelming solidity of the old Inca walls. When earthquakes devastated the countryside in 1950, the colonial villas, with their glamor and contrived dignity often fell, whilst the aged Inca bastions stayed put.

Although the Incas were austere and efficient, they never had the wheel: the streets and roads they built were no wider than they need be for pedestrians – some twenty-five feet wide. People usually saunter along amidst llama traffic. Today the hooting of horns is replaced – in the old parts of the city – by a hissing technique which enables you to make a llama stop, start or turn. Many sewers still run open in the middle of the streets; yet modern Peru has impinged on Cuzco, without overwhelming it. Men in shiny suits carrying transistor radios down the streets are common, but so is the sprightly bachelor denoting his eligibility for marriage by flowers stuck ostentatiously in his hat. The Inca mood of the place prevails over both the Spanish colonial and the modern. Cuzco feels more stone than stucco.

The extraordinary character of Cuzco, the ancient capital of the Inca empire, although manifested today in the impressive power of its stone building, derived from its role not just as urban center, but as the heart of a mighty empire and the center of worship of the glorious Sun God. Cuzco means 'navel of the world'. That was exactly what Cuzco was. Cuzco, linked by a network of roads to the furthest-flung parts of the empire which, from the 13th to the 16th centuries extended over mountains and deserts from Peru across Bolivia into Argentina and Chile and northwards into Ecuador. It seemed, in fact, that all roads led to Cuzco and that Cuzco held all the elements of the empire together, not just by sheer political power, but spiritually. By the Inca system there was no ownership of land; not only was every individual provided for, from birth to death, his life was controlled and his work directed for the good of the state. Dominating every aspect of Inca life were the ceremonies directed to the Sun God. And Cuzco, with its enormous temple and vast numbers of priests, was the center of worship.

Cuzco, built by the Incas, did not suit the conquering Spaniards who, led by Pizarro, inflicted the crippling blow to the already declining Inca empire with the treacherous murder of Atahualpa, the last to reign over an autonomous empire. In 1533 the invaders entered Cuzco unopposed and immediately set up a Spanish municipality granting land and Indians to the Spanish settlers, and building a cathedral and colonial city on the remains of the Inca temple and plundered city. Cuzco was too remote as a seat of government for the extensive area the Spanish had conquered.

Spanish civilization is an urban phenomenon. Even Spanish rustics prefer to live in miniature towns rather than in isolated cottages. The Spaniards brought with them their urban instincts. They were unable to conceive of a civilization without cities. In just 16 years the Spanish founded the most important cities of highland South America: Quito in 1534, Lima in 1535, Bogota in 1538 and La Paz in 1548. Innumerable settlement sites, from rural villages to the imperial capitals of Cuzco and Quito, were allowed to keep their identity and rebuilt as colonial cities. Although often supposed to have been newly established by the Spaniards even Lima in the Rimac valley had a pre-Conquest origin, while Bogota was founded on the site of a Chibcha village.

Among the cities founded and developed by the Spanish there was no urban equivalent of Inca Cuzco. The principal Spanish cities tended to be planned and established at points of contact between the mother country and the resources of the continent and revolved around a system whose center was thousands of miles away. Apart from defense, little attention was given in the choice of sites to factors such as suitability of the physical conditions for growth. Indeed many of the cities were not at all well placed to achieve and support growth, as later events were to tell. Many of the cities were isolated and inaccessible. Bogota and Quito could be reached only by a six months' safari by boat and mule from the Atlantic coast.

Most of the Spanish-founded cities of highland South America still seem uncertain of their identity, often feel somehow out of control. Cuzco knows its essence; its

Like Santiago's cathedral the Catholic Church has represented stability, paternalism and splendor for centuries. Some priests now voice rebellion.

Lima's hillside *barriadas* are
spawned by a population which
quadrupled in a generation.
They lack jobs, but in the
country hope is even thinner.

personality is stable, its identity is real but not over-assertive. Spanish-founded cities tend to feel rootless, even artificial. Perhaps this is because they were built for Spain, though now they are wholly Peruvian. Lima, the Spaniards' once glittering capital of the Pacific coast, is such a place, though it was built on the site of an old village that existed before the Spaniard came.

Even the weather in Lima is hard to categorize. *Limenos* say there are four seasons every day. *Garua,* a damp grey mist, often hovers over the city in the morning, accentuating the faceless grimness of many of the buildings. But it never rains (ironically, it would brighten the dullness of the monotony if it sometimes did): Lima backs on to a precipitous desert. At noon, it is brightly sunlit; at dusk it is cold.

As in Cuzco, personality springs from conflict between two eras. Whereas in Cuzco, the Inca struggles with the Spanish-colonial, in Lima the colonial is menaced by efficient skyscrapers and office blocks. Some influential men have banded together to save the intricate iron grilles, vivacious, twirling woodcarvings on the walls of grand houses and churches, and above all the wood-latticed balconies from behind which well-bred chap-eroned señoritas can watch the world go by in the streets below.

28   It is the people as much as the architecture that give

Spanish colonial styles and
customs are recalled by the
enclosed balconies from which
Lima *señoritas* watch the world
— and suitors — pass by.

Once the baroque capital of
half an empire, Lima, like
other Andean capitals, has
witnessed many military
coups since independence.

Cities of highland South America

a place its character. You sit drinking your *pisco* sour, against a background noise of clattering dice and men arguing over a game of *Dudo* ('I doubt you'): cosmopolitan Lima variety passes by – Indians from the hills, negro descendants of slaves, Spanish *criolles* proud of their white skins and Iberian tradition: the restaurateurs are Chinese; Japanese are mostly artisans; shopkeepers often Italian. Gypsies have come in from the hillside shanty towns. Americans have settled or half-settled, as engineers; and British have been in Lima as traders for generations now, still with their aura of tennis parties and private schools. You would not guess in Lima, the capital, that Peru was overwhelmingly Indian – not until the demogogues bring them streaming out of the hills for one of the great political demonstrations.

Lima is an excellent example of a city planned in the Spanish colonial style to colonial criteria. It was the political capital of Peru and the seat of the Viceroy. It was laid out on the pattern of Spanish towns as decreèd in the Laws of the Indes. The colonial city, of which Lima was typical, was built around its central plaza (*plaza major*). All round it were the important government and religious offices, with surrounding lots assigned to the founders. From this main square streets were laid out on a gridiron pattern with sufficient space for future expansion. The élite lived as close as possible to the plaza. The place of the Indian population however, was in a *cercade* outside the city walls. As the city expanded, self-contained *barrios*, each with their own plaza, were established, although even after independence there was class segregation. Lima is now the only large city in Peru. It dominates the nation politically, financially and socially.

The people of Santiago make the capital city of Chile a temperate place, giving support to the adage that temperate people inhabit temperate places. Most of the time they seem cooler than other South Americans. Even those who cannot speak Spanish claim to see the less emotionally dramatic pattern of life among the Santiagans. Yet the political passions are there. People in cafes vehemently discuss the newspapers. The political alliances are constantly shifting. And there is the usual contrast between rich and poor – sharpened in Santiago by the two parts of the city, though adjacent, being divided by slopes of almost precipitous steepness, with funicular railways carrying wealthier travelers between the two.

The main, richer, part of the town is well laid out. As in most South American cities, there is evidence of ethnic richness in many small ways. The statues vary from Araucanian warrior leaders to early Chilean patriots whose names recall the persistent attraction that Chile has had for British islanders – General Bernardo O'Higgins (pronounced O'Eeheens), revolutionary leader and first president of independent Chile, whose Irish father immigrated from Richmond, Surrey, after an un-

In Quito the simplest way to
get a new suit or dress is to
pop along to the tailors in
the market square early and
collect it at sunset.

happy love affair, and Benjamin Vicuna Mackenna, historian and former governor of Santiago.

Colombia's high savanna capital, Bogota, under its usually overcast skies, has expanded, like Lima, on the grid basis. Centrally sited, it gives cohesion to a people drawn to the powerful regional centers of Barranquilla and Cartagena on the Atlantic coast, Medellin to the north-west across the great valley of the Rio Magdalena, and Cali to the south-west, with its Pacific port of Buenaventura. As Colombia's population is more evenly distributed among its cities, the country avoids many of the defects inherent in the single huge uncontrollable metropolis. In Ecuador the bustling untidy commercial port of Guayaquil with a population of nearly a million, rapidly expanding into the surrounding sea swamps, vies with the country's capital, Quito, over 9,000 feet up in the Andes. Quito is one of the prettiest cities in the world, a former Inca stronghold packed in among its green mountains, with its Spanish colonial architecture and terracotta rooms, and a manageable population of about 650,000.

La Paz, however, is an example of the other kind of city which sprang up in the colonial era – an unplanned,

spontaneous kind of city. The official capital of Bolivia is the old colonial town of Sucre, but the real capital is La Paz, founded in a spectacular gorge just off the eastern slope of the Altiplano at almost 12,000 feet – a breathless place for lowland visitors. La Paz originated as a simple stop for muleteers traveling from upper to lower Peru. It developed, not by any decision, but as an incidental midway point for trade as the silver mine at Potosi expanded. Then it suddenly mushroomed, regardless of direction or planning, into a haphazard undesigned city which by the 19th century had overtaken the colonial capital of Sucre.

The individual capital cities looked towards Spain for direction and inspiration; they grew up more in touch with Spain than with each other. Until the 19th century the conquistadorial adventure stuck to its objective of trade with Spain. The Andes were immense exporters of wealth – riches poured out of Bolivia through Chile's northern port of Arica; a hundred miles southwards, Iquique burst into life during the 19th century as the port for the vast nitrate deposits found in the desert; two hundred miles further down the coast Antotagasta became, and remains, the outlet for one of the largest

33

Cities of highland South America

When the régime encouraged
Chile's peasants to seize
land on the big estates in
the early 1970s food prices
soared in the cities.

coppermines of the world, at Chiquicamata.

Cities such as Bogota and Lima changed remarkably little throughout the colonial epoch and the first century of independence. At the beginning of World War I they were still performing the same functions as when they were established in the 16th century. For well over three hundred years, government and administration, and residence for the élite families with their large entourage of servants, remained at the heart of urban life. No city developed as a center of manufacturing. Trade and commerce were insignificant. Remote and often isolated, they grew gradually on the profits from exporting raw products and foods – like coffee in Colombia, silver and tin in Bolivia. The great wealth acquired by the few was used mainly for sumptuous European-style living. There was almost no need for industry, as the exports of raw materials paid for all the imports. It is only since 1930 that these cities have changed from isolated Spanish colonial towns to Third World metropolises. Their activities have rapidly diversified and many of them have recently become commercial, industrial and transport centers.

The industry and commerce which brought new life to the cities was an historical accident, thrust onto

The golf club in Linares,
Santiago where the elite
gather is evidence of British
settlers' influence in
South America.

The *bombideros*, volunteer firefighters, line up in smart, central Santiago up the valley of the river that divides Chile's capital.

When the old residential area of Santiago on the south bank became the commercial center traffic began to strangle the city.

Scarcity of land, education and medical care, the lack of opportunity for advancement, and sometimes wretched living conditions have played their part. Indeed without true land reform, conditions *are* oppressive in the Peruvian Sierra or Bolivian Altiplano. Yet most of the migrants encounter city life at its worst. More migrants flow into the cities like Lima and Bogota than there are jobs or houses. There must therefore be a powerful 'pull factor'. Migrants live in vile slums with little security: but they live in hope – of educating their children, owning homes and getting jobs. For many, much of their hope is never, or too slowly, fulfilled. For the cities are swelling much faster than the industry. The statistics are frightening. Lima has increased her population from 600,000 in 1940 to over two and a half million in 1972 and goes on increasing annually by 7 per cent. The shanty townships, *barriadas*, spawn across the dry foothills. Bogota has grown from 300,000 in 1930 to 2.3 million in 1972.

There are obvious weaknesses in an economy still dependent on selling raw products to a world market at fluctuating prices. World prices in tin, for example, rise and fall for reasons outside the control of the Bolivian government. And then South America has been highly dependent on foreign money, mainly from the United States. Investment from abroad thrives on low labor costs and high profits, much of which returns to the mother country. The yield from the economy is seldom pumped back into new projects in South America which would make new jobs. Such a situation helped bring a Marxist government to power in Chile in 1970.

So the people who flood into the cities tend to take casual jobs as the best work they can. Petty commerce, street vending, domestic service, lottery-ticket selling and so on, are the familiar forms of employment for the average migrant. Every few yards on the main streets of Decima and Septima in Bogota's skyscraper city-center, you are met by men and women selling contraband, clothing and trinkets, newspapers and fruit. Their earnings are little higher than those of the beggars who have nothing to sell but their misery. The daily markets are full of vendors who opt for the small earnings of fruit and vegetable selling, rather than the uncertainty of intermittent labor on construction sites.

Migration from the country is responsible for more than half the population increases of these cities. In Bolivia the 1925 Revolution and Agrarian Reform, which released the *campesino* from his traditional tie to the land, was followed by a wave of migration into La Paz. In Peru the tragic earthquakes of 1970 which destroyed large rural areas accelerated the normal flow of migration to the capital.

The ostensible result of the cities' failure to absorb the migrants and the failure of industry to set up new business enterprises to create new jobs and houses are slums. There are, broadly, three types of slum. There are slum tenements in the older districts of the city centers.

South America by external circumstances. It did not develop, for example, from the demands of a developing working class in the cities. Nor did it arise from a deliberate policy of modernization by the emergent middle class, nor from a new consciousness of exploitable resources. What happened was that the Great Depression of 1929 and the outbreak of World War II stopped the flow of European and US manufactures into the cities. Many long-established export and import firms went bankrupt. There was a commercial vacuum, which was filled by a tremendous burst of industrialization.

Immigration from abroad accelerated the process. Refugees from Hitler's Europe of the 1930s played a role out of proportion to their number. They set modern commerce in motion and formed the basis of the entrepreneurial and professional classes. The large import–export business of La Paz is even today largely controlled by people of German origins – ironically, both Jews who left Germany before the War as well as Nazis who arrived after.

It is however migrants from highland South America's own countryside who in the end have done most to change the cities. The woes of South American rural life have been exaggerated as the 'push factor' of migration.

Cities of highland South America

South American countries have
fought wars over sardines and
anchovies. Chile's northern
port of Arica also handles
Bolivia's exports.

In Bogota by the 1940s the élite had moved from their colonial *Santaferena* houses round the *plaza major* and established new luxurious residential suburbs on the outskirts of the city. This outwards migration of the rich led to a decline in the old colonial center, much of which has today become the traditional slum of the working class. Migrants live in these inner city slums on first arrival. They are reception areas, with conditions so crowded that twelve occupants to a room is not uncommon. Many never leave these tenement slums, and bear their children here. The second type of slum is the official housing settlement often built with government loans or mortgages. This type is only available to the very few who have climbed quite a way up the scale, moving into a lower-middle-class income bracket.

For the average low-income family who wish to escape high rents and miserably overcrowded living conditions, the third type of slum is the only solution – the so-called invasion *barrio*. The family illegally occupies land on the edge of the cities, under the constant threat of displacement by the outward growth of the city. If the community is not evicted the invasion *barrio* may develop over twenty years into a typical lower-middle-class *barrio*.

The houses of the 'invaders', built in stages as their owners' resources permit, are frequently made of straw, wood or cardboard. They are without water, sanitation or light – though this is sometimes cleverly pirated off the mains that serve nearby street lights.

The invasion *barriadas* of Lima – such as Villa El Salvador and Pampa de Cuervas – absorb about 20,000 families a year on the banks of the Rimac river and on the hills surrounding the city. Half the city's total population live in them. The mountain ridge behind Bogota has been similarly invaded by squatters. The upper classes are alternately charmed and alarmed: they tend to find the slums either picturesque or threatening.

The upper classes have moved from around the *plaza major* in Bogota and Lima. They now live in rigidly segregated new suburbs. San Isidro and Miraflores lie beyond the *barriadas* that ring the commercial center of Lima. Chico and Antigua Country are to the north of Bogota's business center while most of the poor *barrios* are to the south of the city or climb up the mountains behind. In La Paz the rich live downhill where the altitude is lower, while the Aymara Indians and Cholos (the half-castes) have built their corrugated-roofed huts right up the mountainside until they join the shanty-town of El Alto at the top.

A sizeable middle-class is growing, but they are not a vanguard of political change; in general they aspire to join the élite, not to diminish the gap between rich and poor. It seems unlikely that the abyss that separates suburban cocktail-drinkers and slum-families will soon be bridged. For the élite of ancient Spanish families and the commercial new-rich still effectively exclude the rest from power and wealth.

Anchovies, for canned delicacies and the fishmeal trade, are pumped into the hold. Peruvians lead the world's fish product industry.

(Center) Peru has demanded a 200-mile fishing limit for her vast fleet of fishing vessels. A smack from Callao, Lima's port, hauls in.

Cayapa
Ecuador

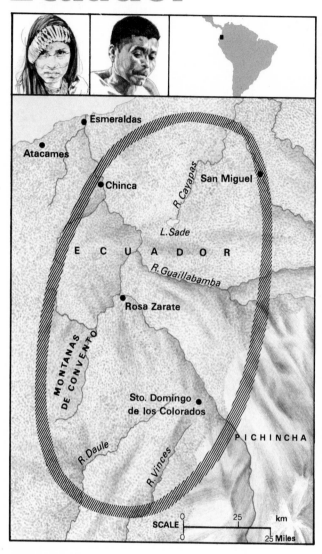

The Cayapas river runs into the Pacific ocean just north of the town of Esmeraldas, on the north-west coast of Ecuador. For 200 miles the river cuts through a tropical rainforest which, for 330 days of the year, is drenched in torrential rain. The sky is almost always leaden; at night neither the moon nor the stars cut a clear path through the gloom. The river runs swiftly, often sweeping fallen trees and logs along with it. And in the forest the mud is inches deep, for the rain does not leave the ground time to dry. Along the banks of this river – and along its many tributaries – the Cayapa Indians have made their home.

The Cayapa village is almost concealed behind a thick mantle of trees. A muddy, slippery path leads up from the river where the dugout canoes are moored to the small group of houses. There are only three houses, hardly a village, and to escape the mud they are all built on piles above the ground. Three or four families live in

The hammock is an invention
of forest-dwelling South
American Indians—like
the Cayapa, still largely
undisturbed by outsiders.

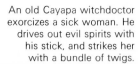

(Opposite) This group of Cayapa live by the Sapayo river in a forest clearing enclosing four homes, each with a palm-thatch roof.

The Cayapa have great respect for the missionary priests who built their simple churches. But their catholicism is mingled with old superstitions.

An old Cayapa witchdoctor exorcizes a sick woman. He drives out evil spirits with his stick, and strikes her with a bundle of twigs.

each house which is open on all sides; a palm-thatched roof shelters them from the rain; everyone sleeps on bark cloth mats on the bamboo floor.

This settlement is but one of many, for there are about 2,500 Cayapa still living in the rainforest along the rivers. In this region, which covers almost 4,000 square miles, rivers and streams are the only highways, and dugout canoes the only means of transport and contact. The Cayapa are famed for their canoes. They trade them everywhere; everyone who uses the river – even negroes and whites who have built villages nearer the coast – buys a Cayapa canoe. The Cayapa men may have traveled 100 miles into the interior, to the foot of the Andes, to find the tall, strong hardwood trees from which they build their canoes. The trees are cut down and dragged to the nearest waterway where the work can begin. A 24-foot canoe, which holds twelve people, will take two weeks to complete.

The Cayapa region is everywhere cut by rivers. It is a region of jungle, completely uninhabited except along these rivers, and the thick undergrowth makes travel almost impossible. The Cayapa avoid the jungle whenever possible, only entering it on short hunting trips or to cut timber for their canoes. Their canoes are in constant use, as the Cayapa paddle along the rivers between the scattered settlements. The rivers are seldom quiet. During the recent banana boom, many other people moved into the region – the rivers were filled with traffic of planters and workers, whites and negroes, and all their goods.

Children learn to handle canoes by balancing on the drifting logs that come down when the river is in flood. From about the age of nine, a child may have a small canoe seven to eight feet long and scarcely a foot wide made for him by his father. At this age, boys begin to accompany their fathers into the bush where the canoes are roughed out with axes and adzes. By the time the

(Top) Dugout canoes made by Cayapa are famed among the river peoples as far away as the north-west Ecuador coast.

The rivers offer only limited supplies of fish, not only because of fast currents but because negroes nearby use dynamite to kill their catch.

boys have reached their late teens they have acquired a large measure of skill in handling and building canoes. But several more years will pass before canoes they have made will be complimented for their finish.

Sometimes whole families take to the canoe for a voyage down the coast. Even the children are expected to wield a paddle. The dugout carries all they wish to sell: rubber, cocoa, plantains and even timber. But these trading expeditions often take the Cayapa onto the ocean, south to Esmeraldas, or north to Tumaco in Colombia.

The Cayapa claim that they are not native to the low-lands but that they originally lived in the Andean high-lands near the town of Ibarra. The first historical reference to the word Cayapa is as a surname. In a document almost 400 years old mention is made of a town called Espiritu Santo whose chief was called Felipe Cayapa. Today, however, Cayapa is not used as a sur-name. It can be translated as 'little father' and even 400 years ago was probably an official title. Modern Cayapa Indians refer to themselves as *Chachi* or 'people', and to their chiefs as *Uñi*.

The first reliable information on the Cayapa comes from a British traveler, W B Stevenson, who visited them briefly in 1809. There was only one tribal group then who lived in the vicinity of Punta Venado in the lower reaches of the Cayapa River. Stevenson gave only a meager description of Cayapa life, for he was more interested in visiting the Malaba, a group of reputedly wild Indians. The Malaba lived along one of the upper tributaries of the Cayapas River, and were avoided by the Cayapa. Now the Malaba tribe is extinct, but their name lingers on to describe evil spirits that dwell in the bush.

It appears from Stevenson's location of the Cayapa, near the lower reaches of the Cayapas River, and of the Malaba along the upper reaches, that the Cayapa's ancient migration from the Andean highlands took place down the Santiago River. When they reached the con-fluence with the Cayapas river they then continued to follow the Santiago. Sure knowledge of their journey can only come by way of archaeology; but as yet nothing is known of Cayapa pre-history. The region, rich in archaeological remains, has not been excavated. The Cayapa, however, claim that the splendid figurines, pottery, and gold pieces found in the area were not made by their ancestors but by the 'Indios Bravos' who were the original inhabitants of the region, and whom the ancestors of the Cayapa drove out by magic. This leads us to suppose that the creators of the artifacts were the Esmeralda, whose Chibcha language died out in the 19th century. The Cayapa language also belongs to the Chibcha family and today their closest living linguistic relatives are the Colorado Indians of Ecuador and the Coaiquer Indians of Colombia.

More than at any time since the Spanish Conquest of

A small Cayapa girl crosses
the river in a canoe made
especially for her. When
even younger, children practise
canoeing on logs.

South America, the Cayapa are discovering the effects of a way of life that is entirely new. In the towns the Cayapa families trade their products of the forest for factory-made things, metal pots and yards of cloth. Some save up for years to buy a sewing machine or a transistor radio; but on their return to the forest, they return to their traditional ways. Only when they hear of a proposed road through their region do they take fright.

When the Cayapa have a problem, whether it is the challenge of a new industrial culture to their own canoe-borne subsistence culture or an incestuous love affair which they regard as sinful they tend to meet it halfway, but not all the way. They acknowledge it, but do not confront it head-on. Major life-changing decisions tend to remain unresolved. In this way they commit themselves neither to accepting nor to resisting the new. Their future, if not assured by their obliquity, is at least open.

In the Cayapa forest there are as yet no government schools, public services or tax collectors; doctors only visit the region for the fight against malaria. Only 50 or 100 Cayapa can write; a few send their children to the missionaries' schools, but this is done more to gain some favor from the missionary than from any conviction that children should learn, advance themselves and partici-

pate in the wider life of Ecuador. The Cayapa are hostile to change; there is peace in the forest and along the rivers.

In their own territory they are largely responsible for their own affairs. They live in scattered groups along the rivers and isolated pockets can be found widely dispersed in the coastal regions of Cojimies and Muisne. But every group owes allegiance to one of the four pueblos, into which their territory is divided and each of which is effectively independent, governed by a hereditary chief called an *Uñi* or, officially, *Gobernador*. This office is passed on from father to son, and if the eldest son refuses the job – or if he is held to be incapable of handling it – the title remains in the family, going to the next son in line. If the *Uñi's* son is too young at the death of his father, his uncle will act as regent, but the position will always revert back to the young heir on the death of the regent.

The *Uñi* is assisted by a *Kasa Uñi* and other officials who have Spanish titles like Secretario, Teniente Politico, Alcade, Captain and Sargento, but each of whom is known to the Cayapa as *Chaitala* or 'one who brings people together'. At the Easter and Christmas fiestas they sometimes gather together to try a case before the *Uñi* who pronounces judgement. They all share one 41

Plantains, the staple of the
Cayapa diet, are first boiled
then crushed between two
bricks—to be mixed with
a little fish or meat.

function: arranging marriages and settling disputes.

In their laws, as much as in their economy and family and social life the Cayapa show their ambivalent approach to the situations in which they find themselves. On the ownership of land, for example, the Cayapa position would appear to be quite clear. Land is valuable and the owner has rights to it. But they do not generally register title to their land as their negro neighbors do and, as time passes, boundaries become blurred. Who owns exactly what becomes uncertain. And then the Cayapa feel so strongly that land should be kept in production as much and as long as possible that the landowner effectively ratifies his right to his land by working it, and by being seen to do so. Particularly when land is not being put to full use, incursions into a neighbor's property are common.

Rubber trees are frequently tapped by poachers who, after curing the rubber and smuggling it through customs into Colombia, can then realize handsome profits. But in every known case where land had been usurped or its produce stolen, the complaints made by the owner to the *Uñi* have been rejected, and Cayapa law has decided that the interloper can retain all or most of his gain. The law reflects the Cayapa feeling that anyone who invests productive labor should be allowed to profit from his investment. In effect this is a warning to the owner of the land that his rights are in jeopardy if he continues to neglect his property.

On the other hand the theft of a pig – which is fairly common – comes within a totally different category. Title to the ownership of the animal is never clouded. Since pigs are not worked like land increased production of pigs is left entirely up to the pigs. The pig thief has contributed nothing in the way of productive labor, and if he is caught, he must either give up the pig or pay the going rate.

Sexual offenses are within the realm of sin, the sacred order of Cayapa law. When the Cayapa speak of people being sinners they usually mean sexual offenders; in this respect they agree with the Protestant missionaries who are attempting to break the Cayapa's nominal link with Catholicism. Illicit sexual activities, if discovered, are usually made public and a punishment is demanded. Adultery, incest and polygyny are the crimes that most concern the Cayapa chiefs. Adultery is the least serious and if one of the parties is unmarried, attempts are made to find a marriage partner. Once a philanderer was threatened with a beating by several outraged husbands, although he was offered, as an alternative, a bride of their choosing. But the Cayapa tend to lay the blame for adultery on the woman. It is women, they say, who incite the men. Indeed, the punishment – with cat-o'-nine-tails – falls more often to the women. It is common for a man to plead innocence, claiming he was coerced by the woman.

Incest is a particularly serious crime among the

Plantains are the only crop cultivated regularly. A woman takes the full weight of her load on her head by a liana strung across her forehead.

Cayapa. In the old days, they claim, anyone guilty of incest was suspended over a table covered with lighted candles and then slowly roasted to death. But now punishment is with the whip. The range of kin with whom it is a crime to have sexual relations is, in theory, broad and described as the *lala bulutalaba*, 'we family together with'. Incestuous couples are always whipped and often this ends the affair; some, however, continue and nothing more is done.

Study of Cayapa families reveals many incestuous marriages and some instances of brother-sister relationships. But the Cayapa resign themselves and say the law has done all it can; further punishment is enacted only by the supernatural. 'Jesus will know what to do with them' they say. This resignation is characteristic of the Cayapa, and it has meant that the range of effectively legitimate marriages has become ever wider. Today it appears that only brother and sister, or parent and child marriages are utterly heinous and not permitted.

Although polygyny is prohibited both by Cayapa law and by the Church, some men still take more than one wife. They know they will face punishment by whipping: a poor man who takes a second wife is whipped far more harshly than a wealthy man. The poor man may be cowed, but the wealthy man keeps his wives and the Cayapa law shifts the responsibility for further punishment, once again, onto the supernatural. A truly determined wrong-doer, they maintain, cannot be handled by the law within the legal framework. Ultimately the Cayapa will accept the illegal act.

The Cayapa have, for many generations, been part of the money economy. But they are not given to speculation and have found it difficult to cope with the demands of an unstable market. Over the years they have survived all the boom and bust economic cycles that have plagued Ecuador: ivory, nuts, rubber and, the biggest one of all, bananas. Their conservatism, perhaps more exactly described as a characteristic reluctance to confront the realities of any problem, has preserved their subsistence economy through thick and thin. Whereas their negro neighbors tend to be more aggressive and responsive to change, the Cayapa were never carried away by the banana boom. The negroes quickly gave up their land to banana production: they sold their bananas only to turn their money over to Indians in return for plantain, the staple food. When the price for bananas was high there was no problem, but when the price fell it became apparent to many negroes that they had been taken out of plantain production only to be made to buy the same food back at higher prices. The Cayapa who had retained their subsistence base, remained tribal peasants with a small market for their dugout canoes. In the short term this has preserved much of the traditional Cayapa culture and independence, but in the long run it may mean this people will become an anachronism in a modern, ever-changing society.

43

The plantains are planted according to a ritual related to fertility. The husband digs the hole, and his wife plants and covers the seed.

Kogi
Colombia

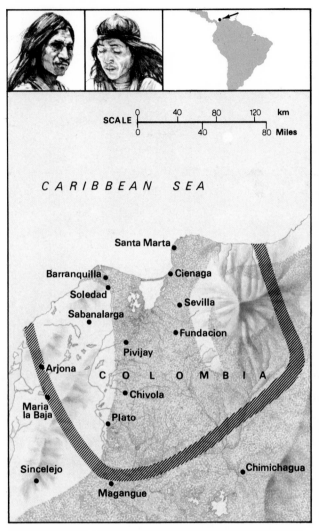

SCALE

| 0 | 40 | 80 | 120 | km |
| 0 | | 40 | | 80 Miles |

CARIBBEAN SEA

Santa Marta

Barranquilla
• Cienaga
Soledad
• Sevilla
Sabanalarga
• Fundacion

Pivijay

• Arjona
C O L O M B I A

• Chivola

Maria
la Baja
Plato

Sincelejo
• Chimichagua

Magangue

The narrow coastal strip which borders on the Sierra
Nevada mountains of north-east Colombia was the
scene of bloody battles during the early years of the
Spanish conquest. The warlike Indians of the region resisted all attempts by the Spanish soldiery to subdue
them. The Indians, who later became known as the
Tairona had much to protect. Their culture was advanced; they lived in large villages with carefully dressed
stone foundations and they were proficient in agriculture,
pottery and metal-work. Theirs was a stratified society,
governed by secular chieftains and powerful priests, and
already developing small, incipient states. The Tairona
were among the most rebellious Indian groups in the
Spanish kingdom of New Granada, now called Colombia.

In 1525 the Spaniards founded the town of Santa Marta
on the coast of their new kingdom. But sporadic warfare,
sudden raids by the Indians and violent repression continued until the very last years of the century. And once
the last battle had been fought, and most of the Indian

The new straw hat will only
be replaced when it falls to
bits; behind their sullen,
neglected appearance the Kogi
lead a rich spiritual life.

chieftains executed, the Spaniards found themselves heirs to a devastated land. The Indian survivors were impoverished and disorganized; most had fled to the mountains. Fields and roads had been abandoned; villages reduced to ashes. Only when a new search for riches and El Dorado took the Spanish conquistadors further inland did the Sierra Nevada return to its former state. Once again it became Indian territory; and though much of the Indian culture was lost forever, some Indian groups have survived even to the present day.

Among the survivors, the Kogi (or Cagaba) remain a coherent tribal group in villages 5,000 feet up in the mountains of the Sierra Nevada. Hidden in the narrow mountain valleys, their round, straw-thatched huts about 10 feet in diameter, cluster about a much larger building. This is the men's house. It has ceremonial functions and women and children are prohibited from entering it. Each of the smaller huts around it is occupied only by the women and children of a single family – no more than four or five people. Kogi family life demands that men and women live apart.

These settlements are not permanently inhabited. Most Indians live several hours away in scattered homesteads in their fields. In the fields, too, most Kogi families occupy two neighboring huts, one used only by the husband while the other hut serves as a kitchen and storeroom where his wife and children sleep. The villages are merely the gathering places where neighbors meet perhaps twice a month, to exchange news, discuss community matters, perform some minor rituals, or trade with visiting creole peasants. When in the village, the men spend the night in the ceremonial house where they talk, sing, or listen to the elders.

Their fields are the basis of the Kogi economy. They are small, family-owned garden plots in which they cultivate sweet manioc, maize, plantains, bananas, cucurbits (plants of the gourd family), beans, and fruit trees. The few domestic animals such as chickens, pigs and cattle, are occasionally traded, along with cakes of sugar made of cane juice, with the neighboring peasants. In exchange, or on occasional visits to Colombian villages, the Kogi acquire bushknives, iron pots and salt. But apart from this small-scale trading, the Kogi are largely self sufficient. In their often badly eroded fields in the mountains they lead an austere, withdrawn life.

In higher parts of the Sierra Nevada, where village fields will not support these crops, many families own gardens and houses at lower altitudes, and in different valleys. From these they periodically move to the cold highlands to tend some small potato fields, then return to the temperate valleys where more fertile gardens can be cultivated and fruit harvested. There is little game to hunt, and fish are scarce in the swift-flowing mountain streams. Their sources of protein are few and although the starchy root-crops provide a regular supply of food, the Kogi seem chronically undernourished.

Kogi men, women and children work together to burn and clear the fields, and to plant and weed them. But harvesting is mainly a female task and most other activities are divided between the sexes; the men weave the coarse cotton cloth worn by both men and women, and occasionally make pottery. They also tend the agave plants which have fibers used to make nets, bags and ropes. The women, when they are not out in the fields or cooking, spend much of their time weaving small carrying bags which the men consider prestigious.

Kogi material culture is very simple. There is little ornamentation. The vessels, gourd containers, carrying nets, baskets, string hammocks and wooden benches are all of coarse manufacture and are replaced only when they become utterly unserviceable. Indeed, Kogi families often give the impression of great poverty; their disheveled, sullen, and almost neglected appearance does nothing to assuage this miserable image. And yet behind the drab facade, the Kogi lead a rich spiritual life in which ancient traditions are the guiding values. The arduous physical conditions, the difficulties of survival, are taken lightly.

The Kogi are deeply religious people. Their beliefs are closely related to their concept of the order and functioning of the universe; the individual and society at large carry the burden of great responsibilities. Although most villages have a headman who represents civil authority, the real power of decision is in the hands of the native priests, the *mamas*. These men have a profound knowledge of tribal custom; they are not mere shamans or witch-doctors but perform priestly functions, taught during years of training and exercised in solemn rituals. High up in the mountains, above the scattered villages of the valleys, there are small ceremonial centers and temple sites where the Kogi gather at certain times of the year. And in the villages themselves, each ceremonial house is under the charge of one or two priests who direct the night-long meetings of the men when they come together in the settlement. The priesthood's influence extends into every aspect of family and village life, and outweighs the authority of the headmen.

At the beginning of time, the Kogi believe, a mother goddess created the world and peopled it with her offspring. The cosmic structure is an egg-shaped space defined by seven points: North, South, West, East, Zenith, Nadir, Center. Within this space there are nine layers, nine 'worlds,' ours being the fifth and lying in the middle. These cosmic layers or worlds are the Mother Goddess's nine daughters each of whom represents a certain kind of soil, from barren sand to black humus. The world we live in is represented by the fifth daughter, the fertile black soil which provides subsistence for mankind. All seven points of reference are associated with a long series of mythical beings, animals, plants, colors, and abstract concepts; and the four cardinal points are occupied by the mythical ancestors of the main segments

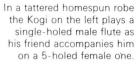

Kogi Colombia

This mountain temple denotes the Kogi universe, or uterus, its open apex a sexual organ through which the mother goddess is fertilized.

In a tattered homespun robe the Kogi on the left plays a single-holed male flute as his friend accompanies him on a 5-holed female one.

47

This area of the Sierra Nevada was once the scene of bloody battle as warlike Indians resisted the Spanish. Many perished. The Kogi survived.

Kogi Colombia

The round, straw-thatched
hut is occupied only by the
women and children, who are
prohibited from setting
foot in the men's house.

48

The Kogi gather periodically
in villages to meet, gossip
and do business. They actually
live hours away in scattered
homesteads in their fields.

(Center) A *poporo* gourd
contains powdered lime from
sea shells. The lime is
extracted a little at a
time with a stick.

After years of rubbing with
a stick, which signifies
manhood, the *poporo*, which
signifies womanhood enlarges
with secretions of hard lime.

of Kogi society: in the North the marsupial and his spouse the armadillo; in the South the puma and his spouse the deer; in the East the jaguar and his spouse the peccary, and in the West the eagle and his spouse the snake.

In Kogi society, descent is reckoned from father to son and from mother to daughter. A relationship of complementary opposites is expressed by the idea that each 'male' animal (marsupial, puma, jaguar, eagle) feeds on the 'female' animal (armadillo, deer, peccary, snake). The ancestral couples form antagonistic pairs. A man's descent group has a male animal; the woman's a female animal. A man and a woman can only marry if their descent groups are associated with animals that are complementary opposites – puma and deer for example. The synonymity of a marriage relationship and an animal's relationship with its prey, is characteristic of Kogi thought.

The great cone-shaped mountains of the Sierra Nevada are imagined as 'worlds,' or houses, with exactly the same structure as the Universe. The temples and ceremonial houses are also microcosmic models containing four layers of circular shelves in the interior of their conical roofs. In a negative sense, the Kogi imagine that the structure of these buildings continues underground, so that a ceremonial house is a replica of the cosmos, and its center is 'the center of the world.'

The universe, the cosmic egg they think of as a uterus, the womb of the mother goddess, within which mankind lives. But also our earth is a uterus; the Sierra Nevada is a uterus; every mountain, every ceremonial house, every dwelling and, finally, every tomb is a uterus. Caves and crevices are openings that lead into the body of the Mother Goddess. Temples are crowned with funnel-shaped apexes, 'doors' which open and connect with the cosmic levels of 'above'; they are sexual organs where offerings are deposited, and through which the Mother Goddess is fertilized. From the highest point inside the temple's conical roof hangs a rope, representing the umbilical cord. The Kogi believe that through this cord the priest, sitting in the center, makes contact with the supernatural powers.

The main task of the priests is to carry out rituals necessary for the order of the Universe. It is because of the *mamas* that the sun follows its daily round; that the seasons change in an orderly fashion; that both the world and its people are fertile. Offerings, to this end, consist of little stones, seeds, small marine shells, pieces of thread or cotton, or fingernails and hair. All have to be collected at certain places and under certain circumstances. The offerings are wrapped in thin inner leaves of a dry corn cob and are then tied into tiny bundles to be placed at a sacred orifice. The Kogi think of all offerings both as food and as seminal matter. This impregnates and fertilizes the supernatural being. If a Kogi makes an offering to the Mother of Maize, she is not only nourished

by his offering but is inseminated and will procreate more maize. A third interpretation compares the offering itself with a uterus; the wrappings represent the placenta, the thread of the bundle represents the umbilical cord, and the contents of the bundle have an embryonic character.

According to the Kogi, because Man carries within himself a vital polarity of good and evil, the main problem of human existence is to find a harmonic balance between these two forces. But the forces, like the mystical animal ancestors, are not only opposed, they are also complementary. The fundamental principle of life, then, is to make an agreement that will balance the creative and destructive, the good and the evil, energies of life. There are similar dualistic divisions in many aspects of Kogi life; there is the sexual division and, in some villages, an invisible dividing line is drawn, even dividing the ceremonial houses into two halves. Each half of the house has its own central post, one male and one female, and the circle of the ground plan is divided into a right and a left side – just as the universe is divided into two by the sun which passes from east to west. All these are vital, opposed and complementary elements of life.

Individuals within Kogi society are obliged to follow many precepts which ensure the fertility and continuity of the seasons, the sun's course, the growth of plants and animals, and the stages of the individual life-span. Other activities, ritually believed to ensure continuity and fertility, are those essential also to their physical survival – activities like the clearing and planting of fields, the construction of a house or a bridge. Some rituals require dietary and sexual restrictions, songs, spells, and dances; the acquisition of this esoteric knowledge is the main objective of a man's life. To perform most biological or cultural functions, a man needs the corresponding supernatural permits or *sewa*, in the shape of stones, beads and other objects given to him by the priest during a special ritual. Disease is regarded as the consequence of sinfulness, brought about by not living in accord with the 'law of the Mother.' All the Kogi periodically visit a priest to confess, in private or in public, all their actions and intentions. Fear of disease and death makes them tell the priests their most intimate problems.

The principal religious ceremonies are performed seasonally at the remote temple sites in the mountains where people gather for several weeks at a time. At the solstices and equinoxes it becomes the priests' task to 'turn back the sun' and, sitting on special seats made of stone slabs, the *mamas* observe the shadows cast by the sun, or its position in relation to certain landmarks on the horizon. Masked dancers, representing deities, ancestors and spirit-beings, are accompanied by songs and the sound of flutes, seed-rattles and small drums. On many of these occasions the priests and the dancers wear ornaments of gold, gilded copper, or finely carved wood or stone. Some of these ornaments, like so many of their beliefs and traditions, are of prehistoric origin. 49

Campa of the Gran Pajonal
Peru

Peruvian Campa of the Gran
Pajonal are habitually drunk
on *masato*. They are feared
by the riverine peoples
because of their warlike ways.

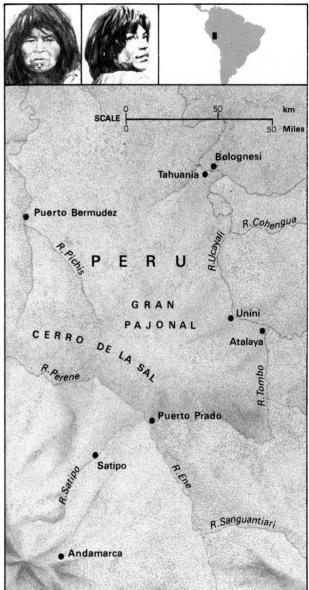

Most of the ranges that make up the majestic Andes Mountains, South America's beautiful backbone, run from north to south and lie close to the west coast. But there are several giant buttresses of mountains that veer out eastwards from the main Andes range and fall away into the vast plains and swamps of the Amazon.

One such buttress is Peru's Cadena del Cerro de la Sal. It runs east for over 150 miles, then suddenly drops 5,000 feet to the River Tambo. But before it fades into the Amazon plain, the chain of the Cerro de la Sal itself throws out another range to the north called the San Carlos Mountains.

Most of the San Carlos range and the Cerro de la Sal 51

Campa of the Gran Pajonal Peru

Two young hunters watch for
signs of quarry. Shortages
of game are blamed on the
'Owner of Animals' who only
releases a few for food.

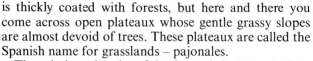

The thatched roof of a Campa
house in the Gran Pajonal is
supported by 4 or 6 hardwood
poles; a simple building, for
there are no walls.

is thickly coated with forests, but here and there you come across open plateaux whose gentle grassy slopes are almost devoid of trees. These plateaux are called the Spanish name for grasslands – pajonales.

Though the pajonales of the Cerro de la Sal and of the San Carlos Mountains are small, they have always been important for the Campa. The famous Campa tribe have for centuries lived where the two ranges meet. The high grassland and the neighboring forested areas are protected from casual travelers by precipitous mountain slopes, dense jungle, and streams too swift and treacherous to navigate. These natural barriers foil explorers, travelers and missionaries, and preserve the Gran Pajonal and the surrounding jungle valleys as the homeland of a people whose way of life has changed hardly at all over the centuries.

In early Peruvian writings 'Gran Pajonal' meant the whole mountainous area between the Pichis and the Nazaratequi rivers on the west, the Ucayali and Tombo on the east, and the upper Tombo and Perené rivers on the south. But today the Gran Pajonal means only the true grasslands.

Outsiders call the people of the Gran Pajonal the Campa, although they call themselves the Ashaninta. They speak a language of the great Arawak family that is quite distinct from those of the Andean valleys and is spoken by many tribes scattered far and wide across the tropical forests of northern South America. But though they speak a different language, the Campa Indians share many beliefs and customs with their immediate neighbors, which is not surprising as they attempt to cope with the demands of the same environment.

Of all the Campa Indians those of the Gran Pajonal have retained the purest form of their people's beliefs and customs. The Campa who have been recently exposed to the influence of outsiders have adopted many ways of the western world, though even in these exposed groups there is still a strong streak of thought and behavior that is distinctly Campa.

The Campa live in small, usually extended family groups, each with a headman as nominal leader. He is sometimes called the 'owner' of the *nampitsi* or living area, either because he was first resident at the site or because he wields authority there. Each group is fairly autonomous, though occasionally the area's most powerful war chief might impose certain obligations on it. If there is a major raid, a large number of men will come together from several different groups to share the booty and the honor. Leadership is more often charismatic than hereditary, although a man's son may apparently have 'inherited' his father's qualities of leadership and authority and be accepted by the group as the new 'owner' without any formal recognition in a public ceremony. A general consensus of opinion decides most Campa matters, but in war time everyone unquestioningly obeys the recognized war leader.

This peaceful-looking child
will grow up to believe that
he is surrounded by demonic
beings who endanger his and
other Campa's survival.

53

Campa life is perpetuated by the way children are taught to cope with their world, and especially with the underworld of spirits. Most important in the lives of both children and of adults is the *sheripiari*, or shaman, who is the common repository of the values and knowledge of the Campa Indians.

The Campa think they are surrounded by many different demons who pose a threat to their survival. The shaman is trained by other shamans and by his own supernatural mentors to control these demons or to seek help from powerful supernatural allies. So for the Campa, the *sheripiari* is vitally concerned with their continued well-being and protection. Not only does he cure illness, but he also tries to maintain the uneasy balance between humans and the various supernatural forces round about.

If game-animals have disappeared from the hunting areas, the shaman attempts to learn what has happened to offend the Owner of the Animals, who can withhold them or release them into the hunting area. Hunters must be very careful to kill cleanly. They must not wound an animal and then permit it to escape, for such injured animals will run to their Owner and complain that

54

Campa men and boys make a daily trip into the forest to hunt; game belongs to an 'Owner' spirit who sends a few animals at a time to be shot.

'so-and-so shot me but he didn't kill me; he merely hurt me!' According to the Campa this makes the Owner of the Animals very angry and in his pique he may not release more game animals into the hunting area of the guilty group. Lack of game animals is a major problem because the Campa rely on them for protein.

Campa Indian hunters must not eat game meat together with sweet foods such as fruit. Nor must they permit a menstruating woman to handle their weapons. Such things will 'weaken' their bows and arrows, with the result that game animals will be injured rather than killed, and so arouse the anger of the animals' Owner. It is the *sheripiari*, the shaman, who visits the Owner of the Animals and persudes him to relent, and to release animals into the hunting area again.

Since the Campa believe all disease is the result of demonic action by spirits, demons, or anti-social humans, curing illness means controlling these agents of pain and suffering. Again, the shaman, through his acquired powers and by control over friendly supernatural beings, exerts a strong deterrent on the unfriendly forces. His knowledge and use of native medicine is often extensive, but his most important function is probably

that of psychotherapist. Many illnesses and complaints of the Campa come and go whether they are cured or not, so a patient and his family put great faith in a shaman, who will claim credit, for example, for curing a headache which has simply passed away. In a world view which sees demonic forces operating on all sides at all times, psychosomatic illness is common. In these cases, the shaman is especially effective in restoring harmony between the sufferer and his environment.

Though the Campa of the Gran Pajonal are concerned with maintaining a 'balance' between themselves and the non-human people who inhabit the same areas, they must also face other urgent problems: they must protect themselves against the weather, and they must acquire plant food to augment the game food provided by the Owner of the Animals.

Campa homes in the Gran Pajonal are simple, especially in the areas least influenced by missions and colonists. The typical house has a palm-thatched roof supported by four or six hardwood or palmwood poles. These houses rarely have walls, though the eaves of the thatched roof may reach down to within a few feet of the ground. Some houses have thatch gables at the ends to

Campa use three types of arrow – a three pronged arrow for fish, the broad tipped one for birds and a fire-hardened one for men.

(Above) Campa spend hours making hunting equipment like this spear. If they wound but fail to kill an animal, it will complain to the Owner.

A Campa of the Gran Pajonal refreshes himself while hunting with fire-water of local make – fermented – from his calabash.

(Above) A straight aim and a firm grip are essential to kill one's quarry outright as every Campa is supposed to do.

With faces painted red with *achiote,* the men of this family enjoy a rare but sought-after meal of *yuca* and queen ants.

help keep out the sun and rain. They never use nails to build their houses; they tie the various parts of the structure together with lianas.

Furniture is simple. At one end of the house there is usually a sleeping platform two or three feet above the ground. Poles planted in the ground support crossed lengths of round saplings, across which are lain supple strips of palm bark a couple of feet wide. These strips of bark are usually made out of the outer shell of the trunks of the *camona* palm tree. The Campa cut them into convenient lengths of about six to ten feet, split them open with an axe, take the heart out and strike the bark again and again. This makes the wood springy and it becomes both a bed for the family and a place to sit during the day while performing chores.

At the other end of the house, they cook. Near one corner, three logs of hardwood butted together make a stove. As the ends of the three logs burn, they are pulled together. If the family owns a cooking pot, they place it over the fire on the ends of the three logs to boil *kaniri* (sweet *yuca*), the Campa's main vegetable. They cook food in the hot ashes or beside the fire. They wrap up fish in leaves and steam them on the coals, or they split them open and roast them beside the fire on sticks. They wrap up, steam or bake game animals as well. They also

bake armadillos and tortoises by removing the lower shells and propping them, shell outwards, beside the fire, while the upper shell serves as a convenient support and reflects the heat. They often throw many other bits of food into the fire or onto the coals, then rake them out and eat them.

Over the fire hangs a round roughly woven basketry tray, on which the housewife keeps her left-over meat, fish and other morsels of food that need to be kept dry and protected from ants. If she is fortunate enough to have a block of rock salt from the Cerro de la Sal (or, today, coarse granulated salt from the mission or colonists' store) she carefully wraps them up in leaves and keeps them over the fire. Matches are novel in the Gran Pajonal, though most families can occasionally get them. They prize them highly, and store them on the hanging shelf. Since it is difficult to start a fire without matches, every Campa family carefully keeps its fire burning or banked at all times.

The hearth is at the women's end of the house. When there are no visitors, the entire family may gather around the fire to eat. If male visitors are present, the men and older boys remain in the middle of the house, sitting on sections of tree trunks, while the women sit by the fire on woven palm-leaf mats. The woman of the house takes

There is only one queen ant in an anthill, and to collect a handful takes a lot of time and patience.

(Below) Queen ants are considered a great delicacy by the Campa and they enjoy hours of probing the nests to find the queen.

food to her husband in a pot or in leaves. He places the food on the ground before him and says to the men 'poya!' – 'eat!' The woman also serves the females of the family and any female visitors.

Each person takes a piece of boiled or baked *yuca* and tears off a bit of meat or fish. These they eat in alternate bites, a style of eating for which there is a special word to indicate that the *yuca* is eaten together with a protein food. Otherwise, say the Campa, the 'spirit of the *yuca*' becomes sad and complains to her father, the Moon, 'they are not treating me right! they're eating me alone!'

Yuca, or sweet manioc, is extremely important for the Campa. It is the main garden crop, and they say it is a gift to men from their fathers, the Moon. Every Campa family has a *yuca* garden even if they plant little else. They replant these gardens, which are near the house, whenever spreading grass makes it necessary to clear new land.

When they have to clear virgin forest in order to plant *yuca* too far from the house, they usually build a new house nearer the garden. So there is a slow movement of families and their houses from one place to another, as their gardens change. But each family usually remains within the confines of a specific territory with natural boundaries recognized by the inhabitants of the area. Within this *nampitsi*, or group area, each family is free to clear land and plant *yuca* wherever it wishes.

The men clear the land together and cut away the underbrush, and then chop half-way through all the trees in the area to be cleared. When all is ready each man fells a large, key tree, attempting to make it fall simultaneously with those felled by the other men. As the key trees fall, they take with them the smaller trees that have already been partially severed.

There is a bonfire of dried fallen trees in August or September, towards the end of the dry season. The logs and branches that remain are usually left as protection from the rain. The men plant the *yuca* though cultivation and harvest is usually women's work.

Yuca is not only important food, but it is important in Campa ceremonial life as well. As the new moon appears, the Campa rejoice that their father the moon is home again in the sky. *Yuca* is boiled or baked and chewed to make it ferment, then placed in a *kahoni*, a long hollowed out log which resembles a dugout canoe. When the *kahoni* is full it is covered with leaves and left to ferment. When the moon is full the local 'owner' signals to all the people within hearing distance by beating a drum or sometimes by blowing a trumpet made from the shell of a giant forest snail, that the *yuca* beer is ready. When the full moon rises the Campa sing and dance, to the accompaniment of drums, panpipes and flutes, and they drink *yuca* beer until it is all gone at one great festival.

The Campa of the Gran Pajonal are feared by those who live along the rivers in the jungle valleys that lie 57

Campa women spit the
yuca they have been chewing
into a trough; when water
is added it will ferment and
make intoxicating *masato*.

beyond the peaks that separate their worlds. The inhabitants of the Gran Pajonal have long engaged in raids against the surrounding peoples. They are known to the river Campa as *waiyiri* – killers, warriors. There was a time, however, when the Indians of the Gran Pajonal were among the most Christian of all the Campa.

In 1635 a lay missionary founded a chapel at Quimiri, later La Merced, in the Chanchamayo valley of eastern Peru. After him came other missionaries of the Franciscan Order and by 1640 there were seven chapels in or around the Cerro de la Sal. From this beginning grew a widespread missionizing of the Campa along the Perené River, and many pueblos were established until some twenty-two missions were functioning.

In the year 1733 Padre Juan de la Marca entered the Gran Pajonal with fifteen newly converted Indian Christians. He established the first mission in the Gran Pajonal on the River Tampianiqui. Later he founded several other missions.

The missionaries brought various kinds of seeds from the coast of Peru, from the highlands, and from Spain. Cattle, sheep, pigs, and chickens were introduced to the Campa at most of the missions. Apparently the Indians accepted and appreciated them until the rebellion of Juan Santos in 1742.

Juan Santos Atahualpa, who also called himself Apu-Inca, was an Indian from Cuzco who had been educated by missionaries. He had traveled to Spain and knew the white man's world. On returning to Peru he dreamed of liberating his fellow Indians from the domination of the foreigners. He finally found a fertile field for his intrigue and anti-foreign activities among the Campa Indians, who were ready for deliverance from the way of life imposed on them by the missionaries. The Campa, under Juan Santos Atahualpa's leadership, drove out or killed the Franciscan missionaries, destroyed the missions, and ruled the eastern forests and *pajonales* of the Cadena del Cerro de la Sal and the San Carlos range until about 1751. Even after that date, however, outsiders traveling through Campa Indian territory were fiercely attacked, and usually traveled with heavily armed guards.

In 1866 a group of Italian colonists settled near the Gran Pajonal. Slowly they made contact with the Campa, and established peaceful relations with the nearer groups. But the Indians of the Gran Pajonal itself have remained isolated and bellicose until very recently. The Franciscan mission re-established at Oventeni, in the southern part of the Gran Pajonal, enjoyed a precarious existence until the Peruvian government's colonization program in that area attracted a number of colonists in the 1950s with safety in numbers. With the greater numbers of airplanes in eastern Peru, the Campa of the Gran Pajonal and the Pichis Valley have learned that raids against colonists will bring sure punishment.

59

Otavalo
Ecuador

At the annual Fiesta de Los
Corazas, Otavalo celebrate
their royal Inca past with
a Mass, music, processions,
pageantry and fireworks.

No matter how far he may be from his valley home in Imbabura province Ecuador, you can always spot an Otavalo Indian. The Otavalo are famous all over South America for their prowess as weavers and as manufacturers and salesmen of textiles. Instantly recognizable in their distinctive heavy woolen clothes the Otavalo are their own best advertisement as they peddle their cloths and ponchos in the streets and markets of Ecuador, and in the cities of Colombia, Chile and Brazil. The Otavalo vendors will even travel as far as Mexico and the USA in search of new markets. They are exceptional for the way in which they have used their traditional skills and adapted them to a modern economy to bring prosperity to their community, while keeping that community separate and distinct from the surrounding Spanish and *mestizo* culture.

Indeed the Otavalo are not only remarkable and admired for their distinction as craftsmen, manufacturers and businessmen, they are also regarded as the aristocrats of Ecuador's Indians. This is partly due to the independence they have won and conserved by their commercial success. But it is also because they claim descent from the Incas. The Incas invaded their valley between the extinct Imbabura Volcano and the snow-

Otavalo Ecuador

Otavalo wrap warmly in their
famous wool ponchos. Although
the equator crosses their
home in Imbabura, they live
at 9,000 feet above sea level.

The wide brimmed felt hats
worn by these boys — looking
down over their village of
San Rafael — are reputed to
last for a century.

capped peaks of Cotacachi in the 15th century. Under their 50 years of peaceful domination the Otavalo assimilated Inca culture to such a degree that the elders among the 34,000 Otavalo who still inhabit the same valley today speak of the *Ingas* as their only ancestors.

Although the Otavalo homeland is crossed by the equator, they live at a high altitude 2,500-3,000 meters above sea level, and there are no seasonal extremes of temperature. Days in Imbabura province are warm and pleasant. Nights are cold. And it is for this reason that all the year round in their equatorial country the Otavalo wear their distinctive woolen clothes. Over a heavy white cotton shirt and loose, baggy pants that stop halfway down the shin the men wear a heavy, dark blue woolen poncho. This will either have been hand-woven at home on the old-style Indian backstrap loom or made in a factory. He completes the ensemble with a wide-brimmed felt hat over his long hair combed back into a single braid, and cloth sandals with rope soles. The women wear under a short woolen shawl knotted in the front a white cotton blouse brightly embroidered around the bosom, back, and sleeves, with two ankle-length woolen skirts, one over the other, neatly wrapped around the waist and fastened by hand-woven belts. They are fond of ornamentation and string many strands of gold-colored beads around their necks and a long string of red or coral-colored beads around their wrists. Like the men, they wear their hair in a single braid, but covered with a scarf.

In their smallholdings scattered among the *haciendas*, the large estates of the wealthy white people, they grow maize, beans, peas and potatoes in their tiny fields, and peppers, squash, cabbage and herbs in their gardens. Usually the small size of their land-holdings, the result of their tradition of dividing inheritance equally among all the children of the family, makes it impossible to feed even the family off the produce. Family holdings are particularly tiny and unproductive in the most densely settled areas down in the valleys. It is only on the high slopes away from the towns that the Indians can exist almost entirely on their own produce. Up here they can grow barley, wheat, and *quinoa*, a nutritious grain unique to the Andes.

But most of the Otavalo have to find other means to raise their living to subsistence level. Many families raise pigs, chickens and sheep to sell at the Otavalo market on Saturdays. Some work for a pittance as peons on the nearby *haciendas*. Some rear cattle. Others become building laborers or domestic servants. But the traditional Otavalo way to raise the family living standard is to follow the Otavalo bent for weaving. Those who don't go off to the larger towns and cities to work in textile factories set up their own home industry, making pottery, hats, or bricks, or plaiting vegetable fibers into baskets, fans, mats, ropes and straw hats, as well as spinning and weaving.

63

Otavalo apply their selling
techniques in any situation:
this woman sells milk by the
glass in the street —
straight from the cow.

(Left) Richly costumed with
floured faces, galloping on
hired horses, Indians from
San Rafael save for years to
sponsor Fiesta de los Corazas.

Determination, intelligence
and resourcefulness — evident
in this boy's face — are what
assure continued Otavalo
success in a western economy.

For the weavers and merchants who can successfully reach the large-scale sophisticated international market farming takes second place, although they still take time off to plant and harvest. These prosperous Indians have made dramatic advances in their standard of living since the early 1950s. Unlike the less prosperous Otavalo who either weave ponchos, belts and cloth for other Indians or simply for their own family, they buy, rather than provide for themselves, everything from food and clothing to firewood. They have come to depend on a cash economy.

Most Otavalo homes, except a few communities near Otavalo Center, still have no electricity. None have any plumbing. Families fetch their own water either from a well which they share with other families in the neighborhood or from streams where they wash their clothes and bathe. They store drinking and cooking water in enormous earthenware jugs with conical bases buried in the ground either in the kitchen or outside in the yard which is normally the center of household activity during the day.

The houses are one-storey, with high walls made by pounding mud and water into a mould. They have a peaked tiled roof and floors of pounded earth. In the kitchen with vents in the wall to let the smoke out they cook over hearthstones with firewood. The other rooms are bedrooms and storage areas. Inside, particularly in the older, poorer houses which have no windows, the home is dark and damp even by day. As the weaver's home is also his workshop he sets up his looms in the sunlit corridor. The rooms are sparsely furnished – a wooden table, a long low bench, a couple of chairs for guests and a wooden bedframe or low cane platform covered with rush mats (or in wealthy families, mattresses) to sleep on. But they have a homely clutter. There is unhusked corn tied to the rafters to dry, and all kinds of things hanging from wooden pegs on the wall: clothes, bits of old loom and perhaps a few lengths of yarn. And there is usually an image of a saint in a niche hollowed out in the wall as the Otavalo are devout Catholics.

The visitor who crosses the fields to an Otavalo home will usually find it a hive of activity. Particularly if it is a weaving household, as preparation for the loom can keep a family busy most of the working week. Out in the yard or in the corridor no-one is idle. Young children help with the simpler tasks, winding the spools for the weft threads, for example. Men do most of the washing and dyeing, and take charge of winding the warp and setting up the looms. When the women are not busy washing, cooking or sewing they and the older children pick bits of grass out of the dirty wool or card and spin it – with a spinning wheel these days, although you can still see women in the more remote homesteads using the old-style hand spindle. Although picking, carding and spinning are considered women's work, men with small

families find that they have to help out with these tasks if the garments are to be finished by market day.

Saturday, market day at Otavalo is the high point of the week, the day when Indians from all over the countryside break the quiet, industrious routine of weekdays to pour into Otavalo by bus or on foot to buy and sell, meet friends, exchange news and drink *guarapo* (a fermented cane liquor) in the local taverns. The textile dealers who stay away selling for two weeks at a time return for the market. And although the food and animal markets swell to immense proportions, the hub of activity is the Indian textile market which is deserted during the week, but becomes a scene of feverish energy in the early hours of Saturday morning. Soon the garish ponchos, blankets, shawls and woolen goods are on display, and the vendors are lined up quietly for the first customers who are invariably the dealers who pass quickly down the rows selecting the best quality woven goods to be sold elsewhere. The tourists usually come later.

The Otavalo have undoubtedly carved out a profitable niche for themselves in Ecuadorian society. They have been in textiles for centuries. When the Spanish arrived in 1534, they were weaving and trading cotton textiles throughout the northern Andes. By the late 16th century however, they had fallen into forced labor in the many textile sweatshops which were established in Imbabura as a rich source of revenue for the Spanish crown. In some regions just outside Otavalo, the sweatshops lasted into the 20th century. Conditions were extremely harsh: centuries of official documents as well as the Indians' oral traditions testify to the punishments and cruelties which Indians endured. As whites avoided weaving as degrading, Indians could improve their lot by expanding weaving activities without competition from their white neighbors.

The reputation of the Otavalo as an élite certainly rests on something more than their claim to descent from the *Ingas*. Their image as successful native businessmen has been enhanced by their achievements as impressarios 65

Otavalo back their claim to aristocratic supremacy (based on Inca ancestry) by exploiting native skills, like this woman selling hand-beaten copperware.

who within a decade have expanded the traditional family-based weaving industries into large-scale enterprises employing many workers. In many factories the old-fashioned wooden upright loom works side by side with automatic looms and hand-powered knitting machines imported from Europe. The introduction of orlon in the early 1960s had a profound effect on the Otavalo textile industry. It saved time washing, carding, spinning and dyeing the wool and enabled weavers to more than double production – and their own standard of living. One very wealthy Otavalo Indian employs about 100 workers, both Indians and whites, in the largest Indian-owned business in Ecuador. The wealthy Otavalo entrepreneurs live in affluent style in elegant homes secure in the knowledge that in the soundest, most practical terms they are an élite, not only among other Indians, but in Ecuador society.

In fact their other claim to distinction, the Inca origin, is in some doubt. Nobody, certainly not the Otavalo, knows who they really are or where they originally came from. There are bits of broken pottery lying around in the corn fields which are attributed to these *Ingas*. And the custom of praying, which the Otavalo still practise, to the mountain god, Father Imbabura, was brought by the *Ingas*, they say.

The Imbabura valley was inhabited by settled farmers before the Inca invasion from neighboring Peru during the second half of the 15th century. We know little of the native way of life before the Inca. However, early Spanish chroniclers called the people of Imbabura, *Caras* and wrote about their powerful army which fought the Inca soldiers. So effective was their resistance that it took the Inca King Huayna Capac 17 years to break the *Cara* stronghold in Imbabura.

The Inca sent in colonists from the Aymara-speaking region around Peru's Lake Titicaca to settle the areas where they had met serious opposition. These settlers were loyal subjects who taught the Inca way of life to the newly conquered natives. The Inca also deported rebellious *Cara* to the colonists' former homelands. The name 'Otavalo' probably comes from Aymara, having originally been pronounced *Uta-Wallu*, which in Aymara means 'House on the Meadow'. The first Spaniard who arrived in Otavalo wrote that the town had originally been called by another name. The Inca colonizers probably brought the Aymara name with them. However, Quechua, the language of today's Otavalo Indians, was the language of the Inca empire for all official business, and it eventually supplanted all other languages spoken in Imbabura. Many Indians learned Quechua after the Spanish conquest because it became the language of the missionaries.

Inca society was divided into a hereditary aristocracy and commoners. The nobility administered the affairs of the empire. They were granted special privileges for outstanding service to the King – they might be allowed

66

secondary wives, servants, the privilege of dress in fine cloth or the use of a parasol, and be carried on a litter like the Inca himself. After the Spanish Conquest, the nobility proved indispensable to the new rulers for collecting taxes from the Indian commoners and forcing them to work.

Although the peaceful Inca domination of Imbabura was short-lived and lasted only about fifty years before the Spanish arrived, the Inca had a profound effect on native life which after more than 400 years is felt even today – in language, politics, agriculture, music, dance, love and marriage, mythology and ritual. In Otavalo, Inca beliefs and old rites and celebrations today blend into the Catholic religious calendar. Time has erased people's memory of the Inca conquerors, but every year the Otavalo Indians' *Fiesta de Los Corazas* revives the glory and traditions of the royal Inca past in an elaborate pageant.

The *Corazas*, Indians from the community of San Rafael, sponsor the fiesta for San Luis Obispo, the patron saint of Otavalo – and so win prestige. There are usually eight *Corazas*, who each make separate preparations. They go into debt for several years to pay for costumes, food, drink and entertainment for the entire settlement. During the three-day fiesta there is a Mass and there are stately processions, an elaborate display of fireworks, eating, drinking, music, and dancing. The focal point of the fiesta, however, is the figure of the *Coraza*. The *Coraza* represents a combination of the Inca warrior and King, always accompanied by a body of retainers. Beside him are two *Yumbos* or forest Indians from the east, and a *Loa* or praisemaker. The *Yumbos* wear feathered crowns and paint their faces white. Following close behind is a personal attendant whose sole task is to cover the *Coraza's* head with a parasol – to protect the *Coraza's* jeweled costume, say the Indians. The Inca had the same costume, but nobody really knows the original significance of the parasol.

The costume of the *Coraza* is strikingly like the dress of Inca warriors and kings 400 years ago. The Indians themselves say that the dress is for kings. The tunic, pants and cloak are elaborately ornamented with multi-colored sequins, beads, tinsel, and precious jewels. The *Coraza* 'king' wears an Inca warrior's helmet, an accurate replica down to the finest detail of the crest's colored plumage. Strands of precious jewels, beads and earrings hang down from the helmet and cover the *Coraza's* entire face and ears. In his right hand the *Coraza* carries an Inca scepter. His long hair is worn in ringlets, and like some Inca warriors, the *Corazas* paint their faces white with reddish circles on the cheeks.

The *Yumbos* are the jesters of the fiesta, dancing and jumping around the *Coraza*. They also play conquered subjects who stir up revolt. The praise-maker on the steps of the chapel exalts the *Coraza* and the fiesta in a flowery speech. The climax is a stately procession of the *Corazas*, *Yumbos*, and praise-makers mounted on horseback followed on foot by the Indians carrying fireworks on poles, the musicians, and at the rear the relatives and friends of the *Corazas*.

At one point the *Coraza* has to demonstrate a warrior's courage when the *Yumbos* and *Loa* pursue him on horseback. At a gallop, they throw candles at his face to draw blood. During the ritual battle, the *Coraza* may not protect his face.

The mid-summer fiesta of San Juan is the most important social event of the year. It coincides with *Intiraimi*, the Inca fiesta of the summer solstice. The festival lasts two weeks: all work stops. The men wear masked costumes and dance in groups from house to house where they are given *chicha* and hard liquor. The highlight of the fiesta is the 'battle' at the Chapel of San Juan outside Otavalo.

The Inca divided their towns and provinces into upper and lower. The upper division was always dominant and 'older', 'male', and 'eastern' while the subordinate lower division 'younger', 'female', and 'western'. In war and religion they were rivals. That the Imbabura valley is divided in the minds of the Indians into these two opposite halves is confirmed by their folk-tales: Imbabura mountain to the east is called 'Taita' ('father'). Cotacachi mountain to the west is called 'Mama'. The town of Otavalo, at the southern end of the valley, is also divided into upper and lower. But this only becomes apparent once a year – during San Juan, when the eastern townspeople band together to fight the westerners. Several years ago, the head of the eastern side went into battle with a banner painted 'Upper Otavalo', so by inference the west is 'Lower Otavalo'. They fight to 'win the chapel of San Juan', and before the battle Mass is said in honor of Saint John. The costumed rivals assemble in the chapel courtyard to drink and dance. Soon they begin to hurl insults at each other. After the policemen who are there to prevent the fight go home, the sides form. The Indians, now quite drunk, throw stones at each other until one side chases the other out of the chapel plaza and 'wins the chapel'.

The Indians of Otavalo are exceptional among Andean Indians, for they keep to old ways in dress, language, and many customs. But at the same time they advance economically and take part in national life. Indians elsewhere have hoped to better their lives by merging with the non-Indian population. The Otavalo Indians, especially the textile businessmen, are not losing their Indian identity. Their specialized skills have lifted them rapidly upwards – but as Indians. The weaver, merchant, or impressario, sees few advantages in assuming a white identity. He believes he can shape his own future, and from this gains self-assurance and pride. Ecuadorian Indians are still severely oppressed, and they have few possibilities of going up in the world; but the Otavalo Indians stand proudly on their own.

Quechua
Peru and Bolivia

Close to Cuzco, on the edge
of the Royal Valley of the
Incas, the animals of the
Incas' Quechua descendants
thresh barley by trampling it.

It is May, harvest time, in the region of Cuzco in the Andes. It is a month when the sky is always clear. The Indians arrive long before dawn to begin the harvest, coming as though to a fiesta. They are called the guests of the farmer; the first to appear becomes the *ccollana*, the boss, and will direct the harvest. When all have arrived, they gather at the end of the field and the *ccollana* raises his arms towards the sky; he gives thanks to the earth for germinating the seed, for having nourished it, for having ripened it. He thanks the sky, too, for having watered the seed with rains. He calls to the great mountains, watchtowers of the land, and then 69 gives the signal for the harvest to begin. The delicate light of dawn lightens the mountain profile; the fields are stirred softly by the wind. The *ccollana* sings first and then the others follow; they all work as they sing.

These are the Quechua people, whose villages are scattered throughout the Andes, in the high valleys and wide plateaux. In their history, like brilliant stars, lie many civilizations, centuries old; and of these, perhaps the greatest was the civilization of the Incas.

Only 500 years ago, the people known as Incas after their monarchs' title *inca*, dwelling securely in their highland cities like Cuzco, taught the worship of the sun and irrigated the dry mountain steppe with complex systems of canals and terraces. The Incas are famed for their highly organized administration of a vast Andean empire, the engineering of their roads and suspension bridges, their architecture, their skill in agriculture and the opulence of their art in ceramics, weaving and decorative metalwork – in gold, silver, copper, bronze, and iron refined from meteors. But the Incas are also distinguished by the fact that they had no written

A llama foetus buried under the foundation of a house safeguards against evil. This medicine woman also sells powders and herbs at Pisac.

language. Their lack of writing seems inconsistent with a people who excelled intellectually in so many other ways. Although the Inca brought schools to the peoples they conquered, their widespread teaching employed no textbooks other than the knotted strings, the *quipu*, which recorded numbers and enabled them to make complex calculations. One legend tells how the king believed the knowledge of letters was the source of pestilence, superstition and vice. Writing which had already come into use, was banned; the death penalty was passed on offenders and the law became so ingrained that many years afterwards, when an *amauta* (a learned man) again invented written characters, he was burned alive. Mistrust of written symbols may have been rooted in the determination of the ruling élite to preserve the secret disciplines of their authority – like, for example, the medieval Cathars of Europe.

Throughout the long glory of the Inca reign and during the years since 1532 when the Spanish shattered Inca power and began to impress their customs, religion and language upon them, the people of the Peruvian Andes have lived by oral tradition. The Quechua people – descendants of the Incas and their vassals – cling to these ancient traditions, legends and folk-tales. They keep much of their own religion under the cloak of Spanish Catholicism, joyously celebrating the Catholic ceremonies which fall so conveniently close to the agricultural rituals of the Inca calendar; they let early religious festivals continue in modern Indian 'games'.

The Quechuan language derives from the court language of the Inca, and is now spoken more extensively than it was in the time of the Inca in the 16th century; it is the most widely spoken Indian language on either American continent. Rich and imaginative, with words that describe complex sensations, observations and events, it is acknowledged as the most elegant of South American dialects. Garcilaso de la Vega, son of an Inca princess and a Spanish captain, urged the conquistadors to learn the language that they might win the Indians' fuller understanding of Christianity. 'The Indians who speak this language' he said 'have their intellects more clear and apt for comprehension, and the language itself possesses more scope and a greater variety of elegant and figurative modes of expression.'

Garcilaso told how the language came to be so very wide-spread throughout the Andes that the Inca 'appointed very learned masters for the sons of princes and nobles, not only for those in Cuzco (the Inca capital), but also for those throughout the provinces . . . Thus it was that in the whole empire of Peru one language was spoken . . . The Inca,' Garcilaso continued, 'had another special language which they spoke among themselves, but which the other Indians did not understand, nor was it lawful for any to learn it. They write me word from Peru that this language is entirely lost.'

The world of the Quechua people in the Andean

The vast condor has always had religious significance. In the *Condor-Rachi* fiesta, condors are captured, baited and beaten to death.

In his felt hat against the highland cold, he displays the inwardness, resignation and endurance his people are known for.

highlands, stretching 2,000 miles from the Colombian border to central Chile, is a network of deep valleys and high mountains. Beyond the mountains to the east are the low-lying and almost impassable jungles of the Amazon's tributaries. To the west are hundreds of miles of arid ranges which decline to the Pacific Ocean. The mountains are beautiful. The gorges between the mountain peaks are often dramatic.

Cuzco, 11,400 feet above sea-level in the Peruvian Andes, was the Inca capital; and still today it is the great center of the Quechua. The walls of Cuzco have withstood the assault of earthquakes for more than seven centuries. They were constructed by the Quechua's forefathers out of massive polished polygonal stone blocks, so snugly fitted without mortar that it is impossible to slip a knife blade between them. One man would work on a single block for several years. The conquering Spaniards destroyed the Inca temples and palaces, but rebuilt on Inca foundations and walls.

Beyond Cuzco travel becomes increasingly difficult. There are a few short branches of the railway; a number of roads, some only passable in good weather. The communities of Quechua Indians, scattered for hundreds of miles through the steep, forested valleys and in the highland *puna*, are often only accessible on horseback, muleback or on foot. The famous road system of the Incas, though paved and twenty-five feet wide, was not made for vehicles, but for runners. They made no use of 71

The Incas did not know the wheel. Yet their 25ft wide paved roads across their precipitous mountain empire are still used by Quechua.

The *conquistadores* brought the horse to the Andes. The Incas and the Quechua had only the llama as a beast of burden — or themselves.

the wheel. Much of the upland is treeless; the days are burnt by the sun, the nights sharply cold. Once the Inca gold had been removed – except where the Spaniards could draw wealth from the mountains in mines, and where sprawling *haciendas* could be profitably worked – the Quechuan way of life was little disturbed, though after the fall of Cuzco the people had lost the core of their community.

In many parts agriculture is only possible with an abundant supply of water, and one consequence of the Spanish conquest was the neglect of the Inca system of terraces and irrigation. The Quechua now cultivate only a fraction of the land farmed by their forbears. But the animals and crops of this high region are peculiarly adapted to the climate; one animal in particular and one crop are especially important to the Andean Indians – the llama and the potato.

As long ago as 500 BC, the Andean Indians had domesticated the llama. From llama wool the earliest yarns were spun, and from these were woven the cloths and textiles for which pre-Columbian Indians are famous. The llama's dung was used as a fertilizer on the barren mountain soil, and also as fuel for fires. Llamas were invaluable as pack animals, carrying small loads over long, hazardous mountain tracks; they needed little attention and foraged for themselves on the way. Even today, the llama and its products are invaluable to the Quechua. Llama trains are frequent sights in the winter, climbing down from the high *puna* to the valleys, their backs loaded with salt and potatoes.

The potato is thought to have been first cultivated by the Indians of the Andes. But beyond its value as a seasonal crop the Quechua discovered how to preserve its nutritional content. By exposing potatoes first to the night frost and then to the heat of the day, and then trampling them to queeze out the moisture, the Indians produced *chuna* – a black, dehydrated food that was light, easily stored and which lasted indefinitely. The potato is still their staple crop, used to make *chunu*.

The adobe-brick houses in Quechua villages, clustered together and surrounded by fields, have roofs thatched with grass or reeds. The women move about in ample, homespun skirts and with striped handwoven shawls about their shoulders, pinned with silver *tupus*. The skirts are worn in several layers, newest on the top: as the one nearest the skin wears through it is ripped out and discarded. Their felt hats are decorated with glistening braiding; they balance them on their heads like shallow pans. The men are dressed in knee breeches, reminiscent of those of European courtiers in the 16th century; patterned ponchos drop below their waists; brightly knitted *chullus* are pulled over their ears like mufflers against the crisp cold. Men and women alike have huge chests, evolved from high altitude living. Their legs grow strong from climbing and their skins are bronze. They are undemonstrative people, concerned for their llamas,

73

their fields and their Sunday markets. But they are also interested in church parades, and in Indian games and confrontations – which can turn into excited battles with other communities – and the two or three fiestas which punctuate the year and allow them the freedom to express themselves in evenings of song and story-telling.

Quechua communities are called *ayllu*, a word which applies not only to the village territory, but also to a blood-related group, centered around the village, though relatives may be dispersed throughout the *puna* and the valleys. It is the traditional community, which served to bind together widely separated groups who needed to trade goods with each other. In the valleys, for instance, the fields tend to be devoted to crops like maize; in the *puna*, potatoes and salt are the major agricultural products. For these Indians it was not enough to trust to trade and barter with communities five or six days' walking distance away; highland villages preferred to own islands of land in the valleys from which they could draw the essential foods they could not grow in the *puna*.

The arrival of the Spaniards and their localized administration broke up many of the *ayllu*. Scattered lands belonging to a single *ayllu* were made subject to different regional authorities from which they could more easily be taxed – and taught the Catholic faith. On the vast Spanish estates Quechua Indians were retained as serfs, cultivating the owner's land in exchange for a small parcel of land of their own. And yet, despite the dispersal and breaking up of traditional communities, despite the abuses and exploitation, the Quechua preserved much of their way of life. Perhaps this is most evident in their religious practices and in their folksongs and tales.

Quechua folklore is hardly touched by Catholic influences. Feast days and ceremonies are related to the seasons, and to family and village life; and the characters of Quechua legend and the spirits of good and evil are represented by elemental forces, the animals of the mountains and natural features like lakes and rivers. After the Spanish Conquest, Catholic priests realized that Christianity could be best introduced by a subtle superimposition upon the existing faith of the Indians. Churches and cathedrals were built, sometimes on the foundations of Inca temples, and the Quechua were quickly accustomed to the splendid rituals observed by the Catholic priests. They became passionately involved

Villagers readily submit to the annual penance of carrying into the town the 5-ton wooden base they have made for an effigy of the Virgin.

and their religion took on a curious aspect, a strange collage of absolution and alcohol, crucifixes and sacrifice, witchdoctor and priest, coca leaves and blind faith.

Many valleys in the Andes are less accessible now than they were five centuries ago. In the shadows beyond civilization Quechua folklore survives intact and ancient practices like animal sacrifice, occasionally overlaid with Christian worship, are still performed. Most often the animal is a cavy, a small rodent like the guinea-pig, but sometimes llamas are killed. Occasionally there is a newspaper report of child sacrifice and although this is dismissed as sensational, the death of a person was traditionally essential to the success of certain rituals. And there is also the old belief that the fetus of a llama, buried in the foundations of a new adobe house, will bring good fortune to the family.

In some parts of the Andes communities still observe ritual disputes over land and borders between *ayllu*. Sometimes the dispute is serious and the two communities line up and fight each other with sticks and stones. Deaths are not uncommon, and must be avenged. This can easily lead to further bloodshed. Every year during the weeks preceding sowing, neighboring *ayllu*, who ritually dispute their border lands, bring their feud to a head. The crisis comes with an open confrontation on the land they both wish to cultivate. The men stand in two opposing lines; their womenfolk sit in the fields behind. The men are now warriors, dressed in leather helmets resembling those of the Spanish conquistadors, their arms are protected by knotted leather thongs. Gradually the verbal battle crescendoes; then suddenly words are replaced by stones and rushes of fierce wrestlers. Should a man of the opposing side be killed, this is taken as a good omen for the harvest.

The Andean condor bird with its ten-foot wingspan is another important feature in Quechua ritual. The blood of this bird is believed to be an infallible rejuvenator in some communities; in others, the sighting of the condor portends good or bad fortune. Two festivals in particular, both involving captured condors, reflect Spanish and Indian attitudes to traditional beliefs. At the Condor-Rachi, held during fiesta time in a number of Peruvian villages, a condor is held aloft by two men while a succession of horsemen ride past, trying to beat it to death with bare-handed blows. Eventually, the man who has struck the final blow rides forward and bites out the

Outlying villagers devote a year to carving a vast image of Christ for the festival of Corpus Christi, and bear it proudly to the local town.

Devotion among the Quechua — one of whose ancestors spent his entire life carving the pulpit of Cuzco's cathedral — is evident in Chinchero church.

The decorative hats of the
Quechua precisely indicate
the region from which the
men come. Designs derive
from centuries ago.

bird's tongue. This festival is thought to stem from the conquistadors' desire to prove their superiority over an Indian god, represented by the condor. The Indians' demonstration of the condor's superiority over the Spaniards takes place in some parts of the Cuzco region. A condor is tied to the back of a bull during a mock bull-fight. This condor, however, is later released alive.

Festivals and fiestas are not confined to those Quechua Indians who live in the traditional *ayllu*. Groups of Indians on the *haciendas* had their own rituals to observe and their own ways of recalling their heritage. In many *haciendas* the owners would let the *peons,* their wives and children sing at night. On clear nights when the moon was full they gathered together in the center of the patio; men, women, children seated on the dry manure singing all kinds of happy songs. Sometimes the owners would come out onto the patio to listen; once in a while they sang too. On those nights the *peons* never danced. Those songs were not for dancing.

But in towns during fiestas, the townspeople sing popular songs for dancing, called *huaynos*. The songs have grace and poetry. Threshing songs are peppery, bubbling with images which seem to be thrown in for the mere joy and humor of it. The shorter songs are pure and unconfused and when they are plaintive it is with

the natural sighing sound of a spring wind moving through leafy trees. Most of the images are to do with nature, for the Quechua Indian never feels alone on a hillside or pampa if an eagle, condor or falcon hovers nearby. Young men and women sing as they walk down the mountain paths to market or to church; all ages sing together as they work in the fields.

At maize-harvesting time the farmers dance and sing around bonfires; as night falls the young children fall asleep on the green cobs. The moon illuminates the ravines, shadows from the hills spread over the cornfields. During the day, in this season, the women bring food and *chicha*, a corn beer, down the hill to the farmers. Sometimes they all go to the town in the evening, through the streets chain-dancing, led by the musicians playing small guitars and flutes. In the plaza the men and women make many turns around the tall eucalyptus tree, singing and dancing and stamping their feet. At such times the *peons* and their wives and children forget their hardships.

Two or three times a year major festivals, *huaynos*, staged by the Indians with their own music, their own dances and customs, take place in the towns. There are small, clean, well-paved streets with low two-storey houses, stores and restaurants; the streets smell of new merchandise and of wine. In these houses live the leading

Men constantly resort to chewing *coca* leaves (the base of the stimulant, cocaine) as a release from cultural dismay . . . and the cold.

In Pisac market the ancient skills of weaving are on display. Llamas and alpacas have always supplied Andean peoples with wool.

Take care, daughters, say Quechua folk tales, not to love the beguiling stranger for he is actually a snake who will carry you off.

Quechua Peru and Bolivia

Two centuries ago the Quechua were declared wholly Christianized. Yet the priest being welcomed at Jarog is still a 'missionary.'

When Machu Picchu, the secret Inca capital that survived to 1572, was discovered in 1911, the Incas' descendants in their huts below could not explain it.

people, the town authorities, the mayor, the priest, the military chief. They are the Spanish part of the town; most of the rest of the town is Indian. On the morning of the great day when the fiesta is to be held, the Indians fill the streets; then, when it is time, they fill the church from wall to wall so that many must hear mass from outside in the plaza. They come out dancing; the fiesta has begun. On street corners, in the plazas, Indians, *mestizos* and young gentlemen all dance or follow the dancers, who wear costumes of velvet, flannel and silk, adorned with feathers, mirrors and gold and silver money. The whole town is given over to the Indian fiesta; even the pealing of the church bells is like an accompaniment to the *huayno* songs.

Folk tales among the Quechua people have a different tone from the songs, and an obviously different purpose. Inca myths and legends recorded by the early Spanish chroniclers told of the origins of the people, of magic beings and mighty kings. These were the tales told by the *amauta* whose task was to implant morality in the people. They were tales touching the activities and emotions of everyday life, using birds and animals to point out the road to a comfortable and honorable life. They bore warnings of terrible fates for those who trans-

gressed. Take care, daughters, they say, not to love the beguiling stranger; he is actually a snake who will take away the family's riches, or a vulture who will carry you off to unhappiness.

The tales contain a mixture of morality and ancient superstition. There is always some moral, something to be learned from the experience of the characters. In one story an Indian girl who lived with an important Spanish man was chastised by her brothers, her father and her mother. One by one she rejected them all for her lover. When, after some time had passed, her mother rejected her, the girl died. Her lover was inconsolable; he refused to bury her. And because of her betrayal of her people, she was reborn – as an ass. Again her lover refused to forget her and she resumed her human form. But then she turned on him accusingly and fell dead; now she was a corpse again, and her lover was persuaded to have her buried. Yet still he refused to let her go. He dug her up and when she came to life, the devil took them both away. His house sank into silence; later it turned to ruins. A desolate plain.

In common with so many peoples, the Quechua have yet to recover from the spiritual devastation of the conquest of their ancestors.

Lake Titicaca
and pre-Inca civilizations

The people of Lake Titicaca
are a mixture of Aymara and
the ancient Uru people who,
centuries ago, were highly
skilled reed boat builders.

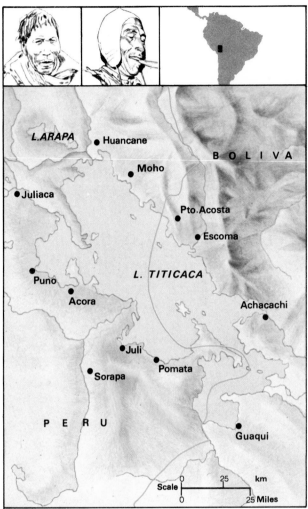

On Lake Titicaca, Aymara Indians live on floating islands of totora reed and fish from reed boats which still use reed sails. These are ancient things that have hardly changed for 2,000 years. The Aymara people learned these skills from an earlier tribe, the Uru who are now extinct, who it is often assumed once inhabited the entire region from the megalithic ruins of Tiahuanaco down to the Pacific coast. The reed boats and their design bear many similarities with the reed boats of ancient Egypt and this has inspired many theories of their origin. But Lake Titicaca plays another role in visions of the origins of Andean civilizations and culture, for here, according to legend, the great god Viracocha rose and spread knowledge and wisdom throughout the peoples of the Andes.

In the central Andean highlands, where many civilizations once flourished, archaeology is our time machine. Its study of ruins and remains reveals much of the ancient ways of life, but this knowledge is always incomplete. Local legends and mythologies which also tell of the 81

Lake Titicaca Peru and Bolivia

Many of Lake Titicaca's people
live on floating islands of
totora reed which are anchored
with rocks and frequently
bolstered with more reeds.

Titicaca's reed boats are
remarkably like those pictured
in the tombs of ancient Egypt.
A larger reed boat recently
crossed from Africa to America.

The fish, which are carp or
catfish, are first sliced
in two then laid out in
the sun to dry. Later the
fish are cooked by smoking.

(Above center) The floating
reed island may house two or
three families. While the men
fish, the women smoke
and cook the food.

past, of ancient peoples and the builders of massive stone monuments, can sometimes help. But often, archaeology and legend conflict; they tell different stories of the origins of the great Andean civilizations.

The most significant feature of Andean mythology is that it invariably ascribes the origins of the sophisticated civilizations to a white, bearded culture-bringer called Viracocha. All highland traditions agree that his first place of residence was on Titicaca island, in the lake. He was 'very shrewd and wise and said he was the child of the sun.' The ruins of pyramids and temples scattered throughout the Andes are attributed to him and his followers. It was Viracocha who taught the people how to build these monuments; it was he who taught the worship of the sun, common among almost all pre-Columbian Andean cultures. Later he sailed away into the west.

Archaeology, on the other hand, discounts these tales as fancy. Lake Titicaca is not thought of as a fountain of civilization; nor are white, bearded culture-bringers easily explained. Yet archaeologists cannot provide either a complete history, nor satisfactory explanations for many of the artifacts they find. In the burial tombs at Paracas, on the coast of Peru, for example, many of the mummies unearthed there were found to have fair hair, a taller stature than is common among Andean Indians and skulls which had narrow facial features. These findings suggest that at one time the people of Paracas were not all like the Indians of today; perhaps these discoveries also suggest that the fair-haired Viracocha of legend is based on a fair-haired Mediterranean people who came to Peru more than 2,000 years ago. Thor Heyerdahl's voyage in *Ra* has made such a theory credible.

The origins of the pre-Inca civilizations – the Mochica, the Chimu, the Tiahuanaco and many others – are the subject of two theories. The first, which is imaginative and weaves archaeological fact with legend, suggests that civilization appeared suddenly, grafted by a non-Indian people. They brought their knowledge and skills to a primitive and archaic Indian world; there was no long period of evolution; cities and civilizations appeared, flourished and died as the culture-bringers moved on – until at last they sailed west towards Polynesia where, on Easter island, many of the same legends and artifacts and monuments have been found.

The second theory does not speculate; it relies exclusively on archaeological discoveries and builds up a history of the Andean cultures, each placed chronologically and demonstrating a development and evolution. We can be certain that, in the 12th or 13th century of our era, when a small mountain tribe in the valley of Cuzco laid the foundation of the Inca empire, it had been preceded by more than ten civilizations in the highlands and deserts which stretch from Bolivia to Ecuador.

Archaeology has established that, up till the 8th century   83

Aymara men sometimes help
with the spinning of llama's
or sheep's wool. It is the
women who weave the blankets
and ponchos.

BC, the lives of the Andean peoples had remained archaic, and unchanged by any advances in agriculture, variety of tools or weaving methods, since 7,000 BC. Then at the onset of the 8th century BC the lives of these people were radically transformed. Maize, originating probably from Central America, or at any rate probably from somewhere in the north, became part of their diet. Botanical research has not yet conclusively revealed the source of this precious cereal which was to become so vital to the Indians that they regarded it as a mystical mother or sister. And with cultivation of maize came an abrupt change in the cultural evolution of the Andean peoples.

From the center to the north of Peru there are remains of an architecture and style of art that suggest a complex, vigorous civilization. It is known as the Chavin civilization after the site in a mountain valley north of Lima, where you can see today the monumental ruins of a sanctuary, a massive building like a platform honeycombed on two or more levels with chambers or galleries. Archaeologists believe it was built at a time of transition when already the principal features of later Andean civilizations were being crystallized.

The Chavin culture was succeeded between the 3rd century BC and the 2nd century AD by the classical civilizations in the Moche, Chicama and Viru valleys in the Nazca region in the south of Peru. During this period urban life became organized within a framework of fully developed states. Art and technology reached a peak of achievement.

The Mochica, the Indians of the northern part of Peru, are known to us through the contents of their graves. In the shapes of thousands of pots, marvellously preserved by the sand, the Mochica recreated with artistic realism a whole refined, complex society. The choice of the Mochica potters, who were all women, was eclectic. They depicted in their pots every aspect, from the erotic to the banal, of their daily lives. They were evidently as interested in manifesting the most wretched as well as the most noble aspects of their existence. Among many

perceptible parallels with later Inca culture, Mochica rulers were depicted adorned with jewels and borne on litters, like Atahuallpa the Inca, when he appeared before the Spaniards many centuries later. The Inca similarities are all the more surprising for the 1,000 years that separates the Inca and the Mochica.

Tiahuanaco village, south of Lake Titicaca, was the center of the Tiahuanaco civilization which superseded the classical Mochica and Nazca civilizations and is described as expansionist. There, strewn about a cold windswept plain, are the remains of a mass of megalithic monuments that are among the grandest of pre-Columbian America. It is a mystery how a people living in the thankless environment of the Andean highlands were able to shift and erect these great blocks of stone weighing up to 100 tons. Copper was known to the people of Tiahuanaco; they used it to make chisels. They were already ruins when, in the 15th century, the Incas conquered the region. Today, as at the time of the Incas, the ruins were occupied by Aymara people; like the Inca, they have no more than a mythological knowledge of the history or origin of this town and its remains.

Tiahuanaco was not the center of a vast, conquering empire. It has been suggested, though not proved, that the town and its monuments were built over a long period, perhaps by pilgrims. Most of its buildings seem to have a religious significance.

At Huari, it is postulated, in a region close to where the Inca nation developed, the form of art of Tiahuanaco was introduced to the coastal cultures of that period. It was a time of change, when the influence of Tiahuanaco modified the traditions of its neighbors. Governments which in the classical age were strongly theocratic became increasingly militaristic. The priest was replaced by the soldier as the predominant figure as wars between neighboring states were rife.

The ruins of Chanchan, the ancient capital of the Chimu – who succeeded the Mohica in Northern Peru – compensated for a decline in artistic quality with great technological skill. Ancient Chanchan, which covers eleven square miles near the modern town of Trujillo, was divided into districts, each contained within massive walls. The Chimu shared their Mochica predecessors' preoccupation with irrigation and Chanchan had cisterns, canals and market gardens. So conscious were they that their livelihood depended on their water supply that it was the Inca Yupanqui's threat to destroy their canals that induced them to capitulate and join the Inca empire. Their pottery, which had lost much of its earlier Mochica vigor and originality, was now mass-produced in molds. They wove cotton materials in huge quantities in factories. This large-scale production, almost at an industrial level, was accompanied by some standardization of taste. This was to become characteristic of the Inca civilization which soon succeeded the Chimu culture. The earliest Inca pottery is poor beside speci-

84

A long plow is dragged
out to the maize fields near
the lake shore. In smaller
plots, foot hoes are used
instead of plows.

Lake Titicaca Peru and Bolivia

Lake Titicaca was the
legendary home of Viracocha,
the white, bearded culture-
bringer, famed throughout
the Andean highlands.

(Above center) The fishermen
of the lake no longer live by
fish alone; the cutting of the
reeds where the fish breed has
depleted the lake's resources.

Lake Titicaca covers 3,200
sq miles and is 12,500 feet
above sea level. The water is
so cold that the lake dwellers
rarely learn to swim.

Two men build a reed boat,
first binding the reeds into
bundles, then lashing them
together to make
the keel and the hull.

(Above center) A donkey is
used to carry the reeds from
the lake shore to a nearby
village, where they are used
to thatch houses.

mens of Tiahuanaco art.

To fill out these bare bones of pre-Inca history we must turn to the mental library of the Indians, their mythology. Indian legends recall an earlier race of men living in the hunting and food-gathering stage of development, with neither a settled agriculture, stable social organization nor the crafts of civilization such as those found among the earliest pre-Columbian cultures like the Mochica. There are legends, too, which indicate that the Indian regards himself as the bearer of a culture passed to him by others of a different race. Often these culture-bringers are worshipped as gods venerated and accorded the kind or respect due, in western civilization, to a Christ-like figure.

Andean legends are filled with stories of white, bearded migrants who first appeared from an unspecified region and departed into the Pacific long before the Spaniards arrived. When Francisco Pizarro discovered Peru his cousin, the chronicler Pedro Pizarro, recorded that some members of the Inca ruling class were whiter than Spaniards, and that there were others who were white-skinned and blond-haired. Pedro Pizarro added that the Inca people regarded their fair countrymen as descendants of their gods, the Viracochas. In fact, no sooner had the Spaniards landed than Inca runners brought word to the emperor in the highlands that the Viracochas – or sea-foam people – had returned. This was in accord with sacred Inca tradition. The people of Peru had no beards, but they had a word for beard (*sonkhasapa*) as well as a word for white foreigner (*viracocha*) which is still frequently applied to Europeans.

Advancing through the vast Inca empire, the Spaniards came upon huge megalithic sites of pre-Inca origin. All had been abandoned centuries before and now lay in ruins. A contemporary Spanish chronicler, Cieza de Leon, writing in 1553, reported: 'When I questioned the neighboring Indians as to who had built that monument of antiquity (Vinaque, near Cuzco), they answered that it was another people, who had been bearded and white like ourselves, who, they say, came to these parts a long time before the Incas reigned, and made their residence there.' Proceeding south to Lake Titicaca, the Spaniards entered the hub of former Viracocha activity. Throughout the Inca empire tradition placed the center of Viracocha habitation on the island of Titicaca in the lake, and in the neighboring Tiahuanaco, with its vast stone-dressed pyramid, megalithic walls and monumental statues. De Leon goes on: 'They also tell . . . that, on the Island of Titicaca, in the past centuries, there was a bearded people white like us, and that a chief by the name of Cari . . . passed over to the island with his men and waged such war on the people of which I speak that he killed them all.' And at the ancient buildings of Tiahuanaco, de Leon says 'I asked the natives . . . if these buildings had been constructed in the time of the Inca. They laughed at this question, affirming what has already

been stated, that they had been made long before they ruled . . .'

According to the tradition recounted to Cieza de Leon, the period of the Indians' barbarism ended with the appearance of the personification of the sun on the island of Titicaca: 'And immediately after this event, they tell that from the south (of Cuzco) there came and stayed a white man of tall stature, who, in his appearance and person, showed great authority and veneration . . . In many places they tell how he gave rules to men how they should live, and that he spoke lovingly to them with much kindness, admonishing them that they should be good to each other and not do any harm or injury. . . . In most places they generally call him Ticciviracocha. . . . In many parts temples were built to him, in which they placed stone statues in his likeness . . .'

There are legends among the Chimu Indians of the north coast of Peru that tell how the sun god Ticciviracocha (Kon-Tiki) arrived by sea, along the coast from even farther north. Most of the highland tales have him appearing suddenly, from Lake Titicaca, as a personification of the sun, but less reverent legends on the coast directly below Titicaca speak of a white-skinned, blond Viracocha who came sailing from the north and paused briefly among the coastal Indians before ascending the mountains to Lake Titicaca. There he fraudulently established a hegemony by introducing his fair-haired children to the Indians as supernatural offspring of the sun. Among the highland Indians, he and his white-bearded followers were referred to as *mitimas*, the Inca word for colonists. They introduced cultivated crops and taught the Indians how to grow them in irrigated terraces; they showed the Indians how to build stone houses and live in organized communities with law and order; they introduced cotton clothing, sun worship and erected monolithic statues said to represent the ancestors of each individual tribe over which they claimed domain; they also built step-pyramids. According to these traditions Viracocha and his two principal disciples departed along three routes: one followed the inland mountain range northward from Lake Titicaca, preaching as he went, while the other followed the lowland coast in the same manner; Viracocha himself took the middle route northward by way of Cuzco. After instructing the Indians there how to behave, he then departed and descended to the Pacific coast and gathered with his followers near the port of Manta in Ecuador. He and his sun-worshippers then set sail westward, towards Polynesia.

The accounts of Viracocha are endless and spread widely throughout the Andes. Almost certainly there are inaccuracies, some of which archaeologists can demonstrate. But where science shows that civilization appeared suddenly, without an extended evolutionary period, perhaps the legend of culture-bringers takes us a little closer to the true origins of Andean civilizations. 87

Aymara
Peru and Bolivia

Descendants of an Andean
civilization long preceding
the Incas, the Aymara
build their traditional homes
of adobe and gabled thatch.

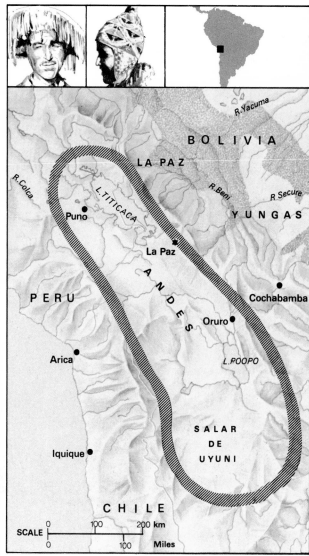

Long ago, say the Aymara, long before the Incas, Indians from the Altiplano found their way over the crest of mountains into the tropical rain forests of the Yungas. In those deep canyon-like valleys which thrust their long fingers into the eastern slopes of the Cordillera of the Bolivian Andes, they found rich and fertile land, good earth for their farmsteads and a nature lavish with vegetation. But they found too that the forest was lord of all and there was no free land upon which to farm. So they set fire to the undergrowth to clear a little space for their needs. The fire blazed and spread through the forest until it was a roaring inferno. And Khuno, the god of snow and storm, as he looked down from his palaces on the snow clad peaks of Illimani and Illampu, saw it too. The smoke rose up from the valleys and filled the horizon and soiled his palaces of pure ice. Khuno was angered. He assembled his weapons, his lightning

Aymara Peru and Bolivia

In the arid Altiplano, 13,000
feet above sea level, Aymara
women hoe fields which will
later yield their
staple diet — potatoes.

Cholo — of mixed Aymara and
European origin — carry great
back-packs of groundnuts by
Lake Titicaca. The ground
here is too rough for carts.

and thunderbolts, and hurled down hail and storm upon the valleys, wounding and rending the earth. The fire was soon extinguished, and all living vegetation destroyed with it. Even the trees which survived the fire were denuded by the force of the hail.

The Indians had taken refuge in caves from the fire and the storm; when they came out they found nothing but desolation around them. There was no longer even a path back to the highlands from which they had first come. They wandered about famished and desolate until at last they came upon a small clearing surrounded by leafless trees in which grew an unfamiliar, brilliant green plant which the wrath of the Khuno had been unable to destroy. They gathered its leaves, placed them in their mouths to stay the pangs of hunger, and immediately were invaded by a sense of supreme well-being. They no longer felt the hunger, nor the weariness, nor the cold. They were refreshed and with new energy they returned to Tihuanaco where they revealed the secret of this marvellous plant to the *amautas*, the learned ones. And thus the knowledge of coca, later to be called 'green gold' and ever to be valued for its stimulant and divination properties, spread through the sierra of the Andes. Coca was a divine gift. To this day when the highland Indian chews coca leaves he becomes indifferent to cold, hunger and pain and he can perform feats of endurance that would otherwise be beyond his powers.

The Aymara believe that they too are of divine

The Aymara have always worn felt hats against the cold and wind. Today's bowler was introduced by English railway builders in the last century.

creation. They believe that they were created by the supreme god Viracocha at the time of the creation of the sun from Lake Titicaca. They have no legendary memory of a migration from elsewhere to the Altiplano. If they were the builders and founders of Tihuanaco and its dazzling attendant culture, the Aymara have no recollection of this past greatness. Not long after the Spanish Conquest, the Aymara, living among the ruins of this city, were questioned about its origin, but they said it was mysterious and miraculous and they knew nothing of its founders. The Aymara connected their many small and scattered settlements, or *ayllus*, with natural features like rivers and rocks and mountains, from which they believed they had sprung. It is written of them that 'they give us to understand that their ancestors are of great antiquity, of whose origin they recount so many stories and fables . . . some say that they came from a spring, others from a mountain crag, others from a lake.' But other myths and legends, some of which were used to explain the origins of the monolithic sculptures of Tihuanaco, connect the origin of the world and the human race with Lake Titicaca.

The Aymara are in fact a people without a history. Even their name does not belong to them, but was applied to them in error. The people whom we call Aymara, who live on the high Altiplano to the east of Lake Titicaca on the borders of Peru and Bolivia, had their own name for themselves: they called themselves collectively *haqe* or men, or by the names of the various territorial groups into which they were organized. The *Aymaraes* were originally a group of Indians living about 100 miles north of Cuzco; at some time after their incorporation into the Inca empire (which often moved groups of Indians from one place to another) a colony of these *Aymaraes* was settled on the southern shores of Lake Titicaca. After the arrival of the Spaniards, the name Aymara was transferred to all the people of the southern shores of the lake – a group which included the Uru people – and those of Altiplano.

Coca was important to the Aymara even in Inca times for its stimulant and divination properties. It has been cultivated by Andean Indians for centuries in the warm, moist valleys of the Yungas, on the eastern slopes of the Cordilleras, and traded everywhere. Like eating potatoes, chewing coca leaves is practically indispensible. There is some evidence that in the old days coca was a luxury. The Spaniards were contemptuous about its use, nevertheless they found the Indians would not work without it.

Aymara men, who are not otherwise conservative in their dress, are conservative about one thing – their coca pouch. No Aymara man is ever without one. Otherwise he dresses like a rather eccentric poor European. He wears a poncho, which falls round him down to his ankles over European style clothes of home-woven, much-patched white or grey material known as *bayeta*. On his feet he wears sandals of untanned leather or of rubber

91

(Over page) Aymara Indians attending a service of El Calvario (Calvary) at La Paz. Catholicism blends strangely with traditional beliefs.

from old automobile tires. When he is trudging over
particularly rough or stony ground he will carefully
remove them and carry them so that they don't wear out.
He crowns all with a bowler hat over a knitted cap with
flaps that cover his ears as a protection against the cold
and winds. His precious woven coca pouch may be
covered all over with jangling coins. The Aymara still
tend to think of metal and silver coins as decorative
objects rather than as a medium of exchange.

The women dress more conservatively, and more
gaily. As the Aymara woman walks the bare highland
steppe, tending flocks of sheep or llama, perpetually busy
with a simple spindle as she goes – just as she has done
for generations – her bright dress is visible miles away
across the brown, parched, arid Altiplano. Her flam-
boyance comes from her *pollera*, a vivid skirt, tight at
the waist and elaborately, fluidly pleated, plain or
patterned of heavy cotton, or at fiesta times of heavy
silk or velvet. The *pollera* is a traditional costume, something between the ancient Andean Indian dress and the
clothes the Spanish wore 300 years ago. Over the *pollera*,
and a blouse of rough cotton cloth, she wears a woolen
blanket doubled over her shoulders, hanging down at the
back and fastened in front with a gilt or silver pin, and on
top of this a four feet square bright cotton shawl twisted

TB causes a high child
mortality rate. A funeral
party buries a child with
offerings of food to help
the spirit on its journey.

Statues of Christ and the
Virgin Mary are carried at a
wedding in La Paz. The
Aymara identify the Virgin
with *Pachamama*, Mother Earth.

into a pouch at the back. In this, the *aguayo*, Aymara women carry babies, and other burdens to market. Just like their men they too wear, perched a little on one side of their heads a small bowler hat of light or dark brown, black or blue or gray felt. Although the bowler, now worn by all Aymara, was only introduced about fifty years ago, they have been wearing some kind of hat for many years. In 1830 a Frenchman on a visit to La Paz in Bolivia said of both the Indians and the *cholo* people (of mixed Indian and European descent) that they wore 'a man's hat, usually of white felt' – in fact a pudding basin hat of Indian manufacture from natural colored felt. He went on to say that 'the costume, adapted to the cold temperature of the country, has nothing seductive about it; it creates an impression, owing to its originality, but does not please; it does not permit of elegant or graceful gesture.' Today's bowler is said to have been taken on from English railway builders of the last century.

The *cholo* women today dress like the Aymara, only they tend to wear half a dozen or more *polleras*, one on top of the other, and all of different colors. The *cholo* woman likes to show the wealth of her wardrobe by wearing it all at once. And her clothes, unlike those of the Aymara women which are home woven and home dyed, are factory made.

The Aymara woman's home, unlike her dress, makes few concessions either to the aesthetic sense or to comfort, but it is no less traditional. Aymara houses, built of field stones or adobe-bricks, with gabled, reed-thatched roofs and floors of pounded earth, have changed little since the days of the Inca. Inside, the family lives in just one single room, only rarely ventilated with windows or smoke vents. There is a single, low door, facing east. The Aymara do what they can to build their houses so that the bitter Altiplano wind can find no entrance. Their homes are more practical than neat. For cupboards there are niches built into the walls with a few pegs driven in to hang clothes on. There is no other furniture. The family sleeps on llama pelts on the floor or on a low earth platform. At mealtimes all the family sits round the pot on three stones on the pounded earth floor. Only the richest Aymara can afford meat, and then it is usually dried, cooked in a stew with *chunu* (dehydrated potatoes) and quinoa. They eat fresh meat even more rarely. Usually the meal is potatoes, fresh or dried, or cereals – quinoa or barley in the highlands, maize in the valleys, washed down with chicha – maize beer. Aymara hate eating in public; if they are ever forced to eat out they eat as unobtrusively as possible, facing the wall. Only at fiesta times when the house is sometimes decorated with colored paper streamers does any gaiety relieve the customary austerity of the Aymara woman's home.

The Aymara have a strictly practical attitude towards everything, including their religion. Since the Spanish Conquest, Catholicism has combined with their traditional beliefs to produce a religion not of salvation, but

of this life, in which religious acts are performed with the due submissiveness to exert a favorable influence on the affairs of this world, not the next. The Aymaras' interest in the souls of the dead stops where the dead cease to have power to affect the living. While they will deeply revere human and divine superiors they are not inclined to metaphysical clarity. The Christian doctrines of the after-life, heaven and hell, salvation, punishment and reward, although accepted as authoritative where they are taught, in the end have no meaning. Ever since the time of the Conquest when Pizarro's chaplain propounded to Atahuallpa, the Inca, the articles of Christian faith, and these were mistranslated by the interpreter as 'three Gods and one God and that makes four,' Christian doctrine has had only a limited influence on the Andean Indians.

Today Christian belief and ritual, its meaning often distorted out of all recognition, is incongruously welded with Indian beliefs and practices. God and Christ, of whom Christ is often regarded as superior – are two deities living in amity together. The saints are worshipped alongside more traditional deities. Even the sale of religious candles flourishes. Yet in the early years of the Spanish Conquest, when the Aymara and the Quechua Indians were compulsorily subjected to baptism *en masse*, their passive opposition to Christianity was strong. A religion which was inculcated by violence and the sword, and whose purveyors were also purveyors of savage oppression, could make but little appeal to a simple, upright people. Although with the collapse of Inca authority, the Inca religion – committed to ceremonial worship of the sun dynasty – and priesthood ostensibly disappeared, the bulk of the Indians' beliefs, rituals and superstitions survived and still persist. God is sometimes identified with *Inti*, the sun; when this combines with the belief that the *Inti* is liable to fall ill (indicated by a rainbow) and may contaminate water and bring disease among the people, curious feelings are aroused. The Virgin Mary is mostly identified with *Pachamama*, Mother Earth who is a fertility power; **95**

Aymara Peru and Bolivia

(Top) A llama is loaded with firewood. The Aymara use them as pack animals as they are sure-footed and can carry loads of 100lbs or more.

(Center) An Aymara woman dressed traditionally in her *pollera* costume and tall stiff hat weighs out peppers in the market at Potosi.

More than a millennium old, the metal culture of the people of the Andes is rich in tin, copper, silver, gold and thrives among La Paz smiths.

Each region has its own costume. At a festival at Potosi, Indians from the mining province wear cloaks and hats decorated with stars and coins.

certain figures of the Virgin are centers of pilgrimage, working miracles of healing, bringing fertility to the childless and good luck to all.

In the 17th century the Spanish church initiated an extensive campaign to stamp out idolatry and in 1667 it was announced that the Andean Indians were completely and utterly converted to the Christian faith. This optimistic verdict was only possible because the church had lowered its standards somewhat. For while most Aymara and Quechua Indians accepted Christianity – or those parts of it which they understood – the old deities persisted in their minds. The ancient *huaca* religion, which involved natural features like lakes and streams as deities, and which was cherished by all Indians under the Inca domain, survived. By introducing the old scholastic distinction between idolatry and harmless superstition the Church decided that *huaca* worship and traditional rituals were not idolatry; they resolved that these things were not heretical, and did not involve infidelity as long as divine essence was not attributed to these objects. The Indian had never, in fact, thought of divine essence in the abstract. It was not difficult for him to meet the Church in this without conscious deception. Among the Aymara, religious doctrine is rudimentary; there is no mysticism; and ritual is performed to ensure that the results of toil will be blessed and protected from the evil powers of here and now.

The lesser deities, the *aukis* or mountain spirits, the *apus* or place spirits and the local saints are thought to be the most directly concerned with human affairs. All community ceremonies have been co-ordinated with the Church calendar. It is on the annual mass of the local saint's day that the forthcoming year's prosperity is believed to depend. For this the whole Indian community saves remorselessly and pays most gladly; it is made the occasion of the most important, lavish fiesta. In all the religious fiestas on Catholic holidays and saints' days, a small number of Aymara men follow the system of sponsorship of Spanish origin and widespread throughout Latin America, and act as sponsors. Elsewhere the sponsors are less financially involved personally than are the Aymara and other Andean Indians and more inclined to canvass support from everyone in the community. However even Aymara sponsors do not carry the whole burden but also depend on gifts and presentations of money, beer, bread, fruit and meat. All these are given in order that the giver, at his fiesta, will receive reciprocal support.

The fiesta begins on the afternoon before the saint's day, on the central plaza of the town or village in front of the church. For two or three months beforehand, dancers have been practising with the aid of local musicians. Food, alcohol and coca have been bought. Everything is ready for the dancing and drinking to begin. Tents are raised in the plaza and drinking goes on the entire night. But the following day, the fiesta reaches a loud climax when crowds of spectators arrive in truckloads, on bicycle or on foot and the whole community joins in. The dance groups perform their exuberant dances; each section of the community gathers in a part of the plaza to drink, chew coca and smoke. Both dancing and drinking follow a ritual pattern, each group greets the others; dancers dance anti-clockwise round the plaza before settling to their own place.

The fiesta goes on for three more days. On the last day, the day of the *servicio*, in the patios of the sponsors they have served, the cooks, stewards and helpers dance with all the cooking utensils they have used during the fiesta tied to their bodies. The next morning only a few enthusiasts remain. They drink in small groups in their homes to cure their hangovers.

Other feasts like the *asuti*, reflect the Aymara preoccupation with nature – plants, animals, geographical features, the weather and human beings – rather than religion. Although natural features some of these are regarded as deities. The Aymara make distinctions between people and the things of nature, but also draw parallels based on minute distinctions in texture, action, state and sex.

In the world of the Aymara there are few things that can happen to the human being that are not reflected in some way in nature. An expectant mother, for example, is not supposed to handle wool or she will give birth to a hairy child. There is a particular taboo on weaving before a child is born; the winding of yarn is associated with a twisted umbilical cord. Her desire for the child's navel cord to dry up is related to a taboo on the roasting of maize and broad beans in front of a child. A child's milk teeth are placed in sedge grass with sharp edges, or in a rat's hole. The saw-like edges of the grass and the sharp teeth of the rat are comparable to the child's teeth. In a case of scarlet fever, the stone from a hill is ground up. This is because the eruptions on the child's face are similar to the face of a particular hill; grinding up the stone is like dissolving the infected skin.

Any transgression from the natural, normal flow of events is considered an affliction or grief-bringing act. It involves not only suffering for a single unfortunate person, but also for the whole community. One event can readily illustrate this. In August, an Aymara woman had a miscarriage; she gave birth to cells that had not yet formed a foetus. Curers, or magicians, gave offerings to the spirits of different mountains to implore them to keep hail away. Although abortion and miscarriage do not cause hail, hail is a catastrophe associated with abortions and miscarriages. (For hail strips immature crops.) The cells, or the unformed foetus, had to be disposed of quickly, buried on one of the two highest mountains in the region to ensure that no accompanying state of disorder should follow in nature.

Yet however confusing to the outsider, the two religious strains have combined into a unique whole. 97

Chipaya
Bolivia

Hidden away in a remote arid sandy region of the province of Carangas live a thousand Chipaya, a people whose ancestry is as enigmatic as the scattered ruins of early civilizations found in the semi-deserts of Bolivia's high Altiplano.

There is only one main Chipaya settlement, at the village of Santa Ana de Chipaya in a delta region between the main branches of the River Lauca, where the river drains into Lake Coipasa about one hundred miles west of the mining town of Oruro. The land all around is flat and the landscape only relieved far over in the west by the once-volcanic Cordillera Occidental de los Andes. To the south the land reaches endlessly into a landscape of

99

High in the Bolivian Andes
Chipaya women spend hours
each day twisting one
another's hair into a
hundred tiny plaits.

Chipaya Bolivia

A witchdoctor — a respected figure — divines by watching the way coca leaves fall. He predicts the harvest and the peoples' health.

volcanic debris and dried salt lakes, some more than a hundred miles long.

It is a homeland so hostile that it may have been a refuge into which the Chipaya were driven by an enemy, centuries ago. The Chipaya live today, as they have for generations, in isolation from their neighbors, with whom they have much in common but also certain characteristics which mark them as unique.

Between the Andean Cordilleras of Peru and Bolivia live two groups of people each with distinctive customs: the Quechua, mainly in the north and the Aymara mostly south of Lake Titicaca. The Quechua and Aymara languages are widely spoken, with varying dialects, in their separate areas, but the one thousand Chipaya alone speak the unique language of Uru-Chipaya.

And then although the Chipaya, like the Aymara, live by simple agriculture and herding animals, unlike the Aymara, the Chipaya also hunt. They hunt waterfowl across the salty marsh-land encompassing their village in the tradition of the earliest inhabitants of the Andean plateaux. The men do not use guns but rely on their skill with traps or their remarkable accuracy with a *bolas* to take flamingos, several species of duck and the large Andean Goose. A *bolas* is a weapon more usually associated with the gauchos of Argentina who use it for

felling running cattle. The Chipaya *bolas* is much lighter but is made in a similar way from a cord tied in a Y and weighted at the three ends with stones or small bits of lead. As the Chipaya *bolas* is both small and light it can be carried tucked into a belt.

Half a dozen or more hunters, always the men of the tribe, have to work together carefully if a bird hunt is to be successful. The group follows shallow waterways often wading knee-deep through near-freezing mud and water until they sight a group of birds, possibly flamingos, feeding some quarter of a mile ahead. The hunters move into position directly up-wind from the birds and then they form a line as much as 300 yards from their quarry. One or two boys then take a long route to a point down-wind of the birds and gradually and deliberately disturb them. Meanwhile the hunters are crouching in line, their dull clothing blending with the soft marsh, their *bolases* ready, held across their shoulders. And so they wait as the birds are made increasingly nervous by the beaters. All around, the sky is brilliantly clear and mountain peaks over 30 miles away slightly mirage above the horizon. The thin air is always crisp in the remote, high, Chipaya land and frequently the marshes are frozen after the freezing night; yet the hunters are hardened to the conditions and will sometimes wait for hours until the birds are agitated and take to the air.

If flamingos have been chosen for the hunt, the men know the path the birds will take, as they always fly quickly up-wind with their flight formation opening into a long skein. No hunters move at this stage; but their eyes are watching as the pink beating wings and long outstretched necks approach them about fifty feet above the marsh. As the leading birds arrive overhead the nearest hunter unwinds, his cold, taut muscles somehow reacting at the right second so that his *bolas* curls upwards with a flailing movement that sweeps through the air towards the flock. Suddenly all the hunters begin to throw and the sound of cartwheeling lead weights hissing viciously mingles with the occasional softer thud as a *bolas* strikes the light feathery body of a flamingo. Almost at once some of the birds begin to fall, a few stragglers take avoiding action and others somehow manage to continue flying ahead to a distant part of the marsh. A *bolas* does not kill a flamingo, but it snares the bird which the hunter then kills on the ground by pulling off its head. At the end of the day the men return to the village, sometimes with a dozen or more birds.

The Chipaya rarely associate with their Aymara neighbors, who despise them and contemptuously call them the *chullpa* people – people who have just crawled out of the tombs – and it is true that the Chipaya today bear many characteristics which link them with the remains of the people buried in the ancient *chullpa* burial houses of Carangas.

Not only do they look different from the Aymara, with broader faces and darker skin – more of a dark

After hours of crouching patiently with *bolas* ready, in the freezing marshes, a hunter is rewarded at dawn by a skein of flamingoes.

A skull guards the ancient *chullpa* burial towers, made from sods of cut turf like the Chipaya houses. *Chullpa* were the Chipaya's forbears.

(Below) Chipaya houses have a stuffed cat in the rafters which holds a good spirit to protect the home. They have one door and no windows.

brown than a deep bronze – the way they dress is unique and, as can be verified by examining the *chullpa* remains, their clothing is similar to what was commonly worn in pre-Conquest times. With either short or long trousers of loosely spun wool Chipaya men wear a sleeveless tunic made from closely woven hard-spun llama and sheep wool with a narrow woven belt or sling on which they hang their keys, *bolasses* and other small possessions. On their heads they wear a domed felt hat with a wide brim which, though distinctive, probably has not been in use for long. Another recent addition to the traditional outfit is a cotton shirt often bartered for in the nearby communities of Sabaya and Escoma. They do not traditionally wear shoes, although the ubiquitous sandals made from old motor tires are now traded on the Altiplano and have reached the Chipaya. Over everything they fling a thick dark brown poncho of llama wool, which although seldom necessary during the day is absolutely essential at night and early morning. Chipaya women dress in a simple tunic woven from llama wool; but they devote many hours to grooming their hair and plaiting it into about one hundred thin plaits. It is an ancient hairstyle: skulls found in *chullpa* tombs often have hair, tied in this way, still stuck to them.

According to the Chipaya creation myth, the Chipaya 101

Chipaya Bolivia

Chipaya are more pagan than
Christian. Straw crosses
adorn shrines where food
and drink offerings are made
to *Pachamama,* Mother Earth.

are the last survivors of the *chullpa* people who were ex-
terminated by the sun. The myth of the destruction of
mankind is common throughout the Andean civilizations. It usually has as a theme some form of cataclysm,
followed by a period of darkness which is transformed
into light again. At this time, the Andean people believe,
they were created.

Chipaya beliefs, which are similar to those of the
Aymara, are closely tied to their way of life. This remains
as protected in its isolation from the influences which
have altered so many Bolivian social patterns since the
1952 Revolution as it was from the impact of the Catholic
Church when it was first introduced to the Andes by the
conquistadors. Although there is a church in Santa Ana
de Chipaya, there is no Catholic priest and it tends to be
used only on the rare occasions when a priest makes a
visit. There is an American missionary who has lived
there for some years trying to study the origins of the
Chipaya language with the aim of eventually printing a
Bible in phonetically-written Chipaya. Chipaya ritual
remains predominantly pagan.

Their most important god is Pachamama or Mother
Earth. Then there are the spirits that dwell in the various
hills, mountain tops and rivers around Carangas. The
Chipaya make sacrifices, usually of sheep or llamas, and
on these occasions eat meat. At other times the Chipaya

Two men play tunefully on
their reed flutes. Before
they could get reeds from
the jungle they played
on stone flutes.

survive principally by eating the little quinoa grain they grow near the village.

Chipaya houses are unlike any of the huts of other Andean peoples. They are round and built from sods of cut turf with domed roofs thatched with *ichu* grass and have only one door placed away from the prevailing wind. The sandy soil of Chipaya country forms easily into dunes. Although short resinous *tola* bushes cover thousands of square miles and make excellent fuel, and though a few specialized trees grow on some of the mountain slopes, the Chipaya must travel some twenty miles to rocky hill-sides for a source of wood. Here they find the dried skeletons of tall columnar cactus plants. They use this wood with its peculiar lace-like pattern of fibers on the doors of their houses and for roof supports, but it is too scarce to use as a fuel. An even better fuel than *tola* is a strangely compressed member of the parsley family, *yareta*, which grows like a thick green cushion on rocks high in the mountains. *Yareta* is highly resinous and very hard and makes an excellent substitute for wood, but as it takes many years to grow and is in great demand, there is never enough of it.

Whenever the Chipaya build a new house they sacrifice a sheep and splash its blood across the walls and roof. When the family move in they place in the rafters a stuffed Andean cat, which they believe holds a good spirit which will protect the home. Like the Aymara and most Quechua, the Chipaya use coca, the dried leaves of the coca plant that grows in the warm valleys of the eastern Andes. Both men and women carry coca in small woolen pouches and chew it to release small quantities of cocaine, a stimulant which lessens the effect of cold and altitude. Coca leaves are also used for divination purposes in much the same way as fortune-tellers use tea leaves. Divinations whether with coca leaves or with the entrails of a sacrificed animal, are usually performed by a witchdoctor. He uses his knowledge to retain power in the tribe. Most animals have a purpose in native magic and the blood of the flamingos is reputedly a cure for tuberculosis.

Today the Chipaya are undoubtedly unique. But up till the late 1940s there existed the Uru, a people well documented soon after the Spanish Conquest. One chronicler of the late 16th century, Padre Acosta, wrote 'The Uru be such dull and brutish people as they esteeme not themselves men. It is reported of them that being demanded of what nation they were, they answered that they were not men but Uru, as it were some kind of Beastes.' The Uru, who for all Acosta's doubts would seem indeed to have been men, had much in common with Chipaya. They too were hunters, refugees from the Aymara. Some of the Uru lived on reed rafts on Lake Titicaca and the now dry Lake Poopo in much the same way as a group of Aymara, often called Uru, live on Lake Titicaca today. Others lived in the region bordering the River Desaguadero in round houses built in a style

very similar to the unique Chipaya houses today. There are remains of round-houses in Chipaya country, in Uru country along the River Desaguadero, and also in old Aymara villages such as Collana at the foot of Mount Illimani.

It is possible that the Chipaya-style round-houses had their origins among similar houses that were typical one thousand years ago when the ancient Colla people dominated the region of Lake Titicaca. Chipaya origins, although elusive are certainly from some time in the distant Andean past. They might have been separated from the Colla, and forced into isolation by a feud. The Uru-Chipaya language, which only the Chipaya now speak, is closely related to Puquina, an ancient tongue of the Colla people of the southern Andes, of which the extinct Uru also spoke a form. Clues to the true ancestry of the Chipaya are disappearing, and according to the discovery of an American missionary linguist of similarities between Chipaya and the Mayan language of Central America, may be quite complex. It is possible that the origin of these shy, individualistic hunters of the Altiplano, of whom now only one thousand remain, may always elude us.

A Chipaya belt — useful for hanging keys, *bolas* and other small items, is woven from llama wool. It is made only when the old one is worn out.

Tin miners
Bolivia

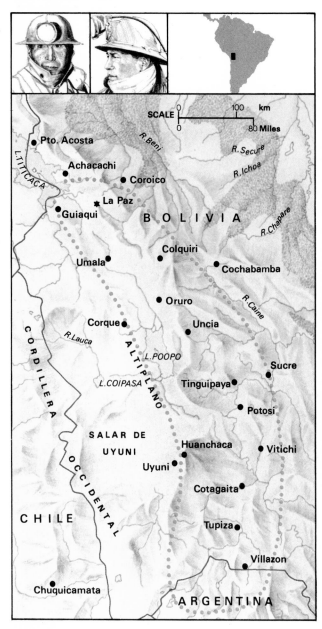

Tin mining belt

Myths and fairy-stories often tell of some fortunate adventurer who discovers a miraculous mountain of gold. When the Spanish conquerors first came to Bolivia, they had almost exactly that kind of good fortune. At Potosí – which lies high up on the Altiplano, the high plateau of that country – they discovered a 3,000 foot mountain composed almost entirely of high-grade mineral ore, and especially of silver.

They named the mountain the Cerro Rico, the Hill of Wealth; and in April 1545 they began mining. It was not their first windfall: already they had discovered the gold

04

Tin mining in the high
Altiplano sustains Bolivia's
economy but the miners'
rewards are small and the
standard of living is low.

and the precious artifacts of the Aztecs in Mexico and the Incas in Peru. But that was a once-and-for-all operation; together with less spectacular mineral resources in other parts of Bolivia, the Cerro Rico looked like providing a steady source of income for a long time.

Although the silver was easy to work, there were other practical difficulties: the altitude of the mining area, 14,000 to 16,000 feet, was almost unendurable. Indians who were accustomed to the thin air had developed the barrel-chest that characterizes some highland people, but the Europeans were quickly exhausted. Transport in that mountainous region was also slow and difficult. The Spaniards recruited their labor force from the Aymara and Quechua Indians, a people well adapted to the land and the altitude, who were survivors from the Inca empire and descendants of an ancient pre-Colombian civilization of which little is known.

So Potosí began to prosper, and on a lavish scale. By the middle of the 17th century it was the largest city in the New World, with over 160,000 inhabitants. More than a hundred churches were built, many magnificent palaces and the finest theater to be found outside Spain. But this prosperity could not last. The silver, so easy to mine, was soon finished. All that had been mined was used to finance the clumsy political ambitions of the Castilian kings. And as the supply dwindled, Potosí also

declined from its early splendor. By 1900 it was nothing but a small remote town, though still an astonishing treasure-house of Spanish colonial art and architecture.

But alongside the silver, there had always been other minerals, including tin, which the Spaniards had ignored. Early in the 20th century, the rising world demand for tin brought a new source of wealth. Potosí and many other mining towns took on a new lease of life. Their prosperity has continued, and today the Bolivian economy is based on minerals which now account for 96 per cent of the country's exports. Tin is by far the most important of their minerals: about 14 per cent of the world's total production comes from Bolivia.

It is of course, still mined by the Indians: the Aymara and Quechua peoples. But the conditions under which they work and live may make them yearn for the old days of Inca domination. In those times, long ago, there had also been mining for gold and silver in the great mountains. But in the egalitarian society of the Incas, where only the Inca himself was above others, Indians who worked in the mines also continued to work in their fields and tend their animals. Mining was not their only means of life, as it has become for miners today. Their present condition is not fortunate: despite the wealth discovered in the mountains, they are extremely poor and lead oppressive lives.

This is characteristic of Bolivia where, out of a population of 4,300,000, the vast majority are Indians living close to the subsistence level. Poverty is aggravated by the severity of the climate and the harsh barrenness of the soil. Many of these peasant farmers, and many of the tin miners, take refuge from their hard life, from hunger and from the mountain sickness, by chewing coca leaves. Their lips, stained green, are constantly moving as the cocaine from the leaves dulls their senses and removes many of their cares. Their manner has become long-suffering and impassive. Women, dressed in brilliantly-colored woollen skirts and shawls, wear hats just the same as the men – bowler hats, said to be imitations of those worn by the British engineers who once came to build railways in Bolivia.

The miners are a shifting population of predominantly young men. This is partly because they have a low expectation of life and seldom reach old age, and partly because the hardships of the work and life call for youthful stamina. But the Indians have another motive for starting work in the mines at an early age, even if they do not continue in them for life. Three times in his life, despite his own poverty and that of his people, each Indian is expected by tradition to give a feast to the entire village of his origin. He must give the first feast before he marries; and since it will cost him three years' wages, he needs to start young. Much of the work in the Cerro Rico is done by 16-year-olds. He will give the second feast in middle life; and the third – if the miner lives long enough – will mark his retirement from active working

At Colquiri a miner paints 'El Tio' (the Uncle) – a devilish figure set up in the mining galleries who serves as a protective demon.

While taking a break two
miners boost their morale
by chewing coca leaves
which yield small quantities
of cocaine.

life, and may well be a modest affair, to be financed by
the very modest income of a farmer.

The Cerro Rico today is still the mountain of mineral
wealth. It is honeycombed with workings, some 3,000 of
them, each one ramifying into numerous distinct galleries
at different levels. It is a geological freak: none of the
adjacent mountains has more than an occasional streak
of ore. Even the tailings of silver, left behind by the
Spaniards, can assay at 25 per cent; and there is an
almost unlimited quantity of tin to be mined together
with smaller quantities of iron, copper, bismuth, tungsten
and a little gold.

Here and there, some of the ores are found in a soft
orange clay which can be scooped out by hand. But often
there has to be blasting, and usually a pneumatic drill,
which screams and batters its way into the solid rock.
The noise shatters the nerves; the dust rises so thickly
that streams of water are needed to keep it down, the
miners have to protect themselves with raincoats. In the
deeper and hotter mines and galleries, they wear only
loin-cloths. The combination of heat, humidity and the
screaming of the drill means that a man can seldom work
at the rock-face for more than five minutes at a time.

For the visitor who knows that he can soon get away,
the scene can be fascinating. He will be given a plastic

Behind a miner's hard-working
wife, photos tell the story
of a poor boy in Rio de
Janeiro to whom this generous
family tried to send money.

Tin miners Bolivia

In see-saw fashion two gleaners arduously crush ore in a home-made rocker. It takes a long time and the output is small.

To try and get even more ore the gleaners put the tailings through a water sluice of primitive design.

Juan and Pedro pray in the cemetery for their father who perished in the mine. In their little carts they have brought flowers.

helmet and a head-lamp, and be told to go cautiously, since uninsulated power-cables run along the low roofs of many of the galleries. From time to time he will flatten himself against the wall as a trainload of miners or of ore goes rattling by in the darkness, which is only broken when lights flicker in the distance obscured by dust, indicating where yet more wealth is being extracted from Cerro Rico, the Hill of Wealth. Occasionally, the visitor's eye will be caught by a spark of purest blue, as the light catches a stalactite of copper sulphate.

The offices and ancillary services of the miners are all located within the Cerro Rico. One cavern is the engineer's office; another is a store for tools, and another for explosives. There will also probably be a chapel. By Latin-American standards, Bolivia is a strongly Catholic country. But the visitor may also see one curious instance of religious tolerance. Somewhere near the Catholic chapel, there is often another shrine, where the image of an idol or a devil is mounted and adorned and honored. Cigarettes sometimes burn before it as votive lights; it bears witness to the older elements in the Indians' syncretic religion.

The miners now work an eight-hour day; when this is over, some of them show a curious reluctance to leave their galleries, remaining there in the darkness – to cook and eat, to conduct meetings, and to console themselves with *aguardiente*, a potent raw cane alcohol. The warmth and the company, even in these dark tunnels, is preferable to the bleakness of life outside. An American or European miner would only work in these conditions for a handsome wage, sufficient to give him a reasonable degree of comfort at home: the Bolivian tin-miner earns no more than eight or nine US dollars a week – or about half as much if he is one of the *particulares*, the men who work independently.

The miners live in low huts – a single windowless room built of adobe bricks, with a roof of corrugated iron. Their huts are laid out in rows, or staggered up a hillside, and at Potosí amount to a shanty-town that contrasts oddly with the mellow beauty of the old Spanish quarter, with its baroque churches, ironwork balconies and decorative wooden shutters. The miners who live in that shanty-town spend their wages at the *pulperia*, the local co-operative, making every peso count. At night the temperature often falls below freezing-point but oil is too expensive to be used for heating, and is kept strictly for cooking.

It is a hard life, and it takes its toll: more than 60 per cent of the miners have tuberculosis, only half of their babies survive their first year, and the remainder have a life-expectancy of only 35 years. The miners' fare is poor and often meager. The average Bolivian eats less than a quarter of the meat eaten by an Argentinian, and less than one-sixth of the bread eaten by a Chilean. The trouble is that the wealth of the mines always passed through the miners' hands and out of the country. In

colonial days, it was siphoned off to serve the avarice and ambition of Spain.

More recently, during the great expansion of tin-mining in the 20th century, the great bulk of it passed into the hands of three families, the 'tin barons,' who spent and invested most of it abroad, instead of plowing it back into their own country's economy. The miners – who had retained some measure of independence and dignity during the colonial period – were exploited as thoroughly as any proletariat was ever exploited. The knowledge that the fruits of their labor were being sent abroad to support the extravagance of a very few fired them with revolutionary ardor, and in 1952, the popular leader Paz Esteussoro nationalized the mines. The miners were rewarded with low-cost supplies, medical aid and a shorter working week. Yet this radical change did not achieve all that had been hoped. This was partly because of the drop in world demand for tin, coupled with keen competition from other tin-producing countries. As elsewhere in Latin America, the Bolivian economy has the vulnerability that comes from too much dependence upon a single commodity. In Chile it is copper, in Venezuela it is oil, in Brazil it is coffee, in Cuba it is sugar.

The State Mining Corporation (Comibol) also proved remarkably inefficient; management and discipline were poor; costs rose, and were inflated by excessive bureaucracy; productivity fell; and there was no capital for the large-scale investment that might have helped. That fairy-tale hill of gold had been shipped overseas, and there was nothing to replace it. The dissatisfaction of the miners has more than once led to bloody conflicts with the authorities: by the late 1960s, professional revolutionaries like Che Guevara and Régis Debray were attempting – albeit vainly – to stir Bolivia's miners into a new rebellion.

Bolivia has a population of less than eight people to the square mile, but it cannot feed itself or even balance its budget. Perhaps its best hope lies in the agricultural development of the valleys and lowlands to the east of the Andes and the Altiplano, where there is great potential for cattle-farming and for rice, coffee, sugar, and citrus fruits. But the Indians are reluctant to change their way of life; and those adapted to life at high altitudes find it physiologically impossible to adjust to the climate and air of lower-lying regions.

The paradox remains: a country inhabited by one of the most long-suffering and phlegmatic of peoples who have nevertheless seen almost 200 revolutions since Spanish colonial rule ended in 1825. There is a further irony in the fact that Bolivia might expect to benefit from international tension. They provide the only significant source of tin in the western hemisphere, and, at a time of crisis could be assiduously cultivated by the Americans. Until then, it seems likely that Bolivian tin miners will have to sweat and suffer.

People of Tierra del Fuego
Chile and Argentina

One legend that tells of the world's creation says that when God had finished making the five main continents He sneezed and spat. What He spat out was the disorderly chain of islands that makes up Tierra del Fuego. A Scottish scientist was told this story by a friend in Buenos Aires, who advised him on no account to go down to Tierra del Fuego, as it was one of the most inhospitable places in the world. But the Scotsman was determined to go, and went. A mere few weeks later, shamefaced, he sent a telegram back to his friend in Buenos Aires: 'I wish He'd never spat.'

Not everyone has found the land so unattractive. But no-one denies that it is certainly one of the wildest and most desolate places that man has ever inhabited. One of the few men to learn almost all there is to know about it, Lucas Bridges, who grew to love the land and its indigenous Indians alike, called it 'the uttermost part of the earth.' Whether you like it or not, there is an overwhelming feeling on Tierra del Fuego that you are at the very end of the road.

The gale really does shriek – incessantly. The waves sound like a relentless battery of guns. Sailors can rarely see their way, and from the days of Magellan and Drake, they have shrunk from sailing round the southern tip of Tierra del Fuego, preferring the less hazardous but by no means friendly Straits of Magellan. The myriad channels that cut through Tierra del Fuego are no safer; in this puzzling labyrinth of stormy waterways, even veterans of the South American seas get easily lost.

It is always cold. 'A land stark with eternal cold' Magellan called it. Once there were forests that gave some shelter against the wind. Now they have almost all been cut down, to increase the ranchers' grazing lands. You can ride across mile upon mile of land littered with untidily uprooted treestumps that only add to the feeling of emptiness. The winter days are viciously cold, and the nights are long; there are but a few hours of daylight. But even in summer the weather is bitter. Two of Captain Cook's crew stayed out one summer night in 1769, and died of exposure.

To swim is to court disaster, though the women of the Yahgan Indians were practised swimmers and even divers. Endless strands of kelp just under the water, some of them 100 feet long, act as a breakwater and a natural mooring for boats – but many reckless swimmers have been quickly entangled in them and have drowned. And the temperature of the water is low enough to kill most shipwrecked swimmers, even in summer.

Tierra del Fuego is a land where there are more reminders of people than people themselves. The coastline is dotted with wrecks, but you rarely see a sailor go by. There are thousands of sheep, but few shepherds. There is smoke, but the men that make the fire are harder to find. The animals of Tierra del Fuego have learnt to make themselves scarce, for almost all are hunted.

Most common of the larger beasts is the guanaco,

111

When white men reached
Tierra del Fuego, they brought
clothes, which meant disease,
and a culture that swamped the
last Indians' spirit.

People of Tierra del Fuego Chile and Argentina

which is said to have the neigh of a horse, the wool of a sheep, the neck of a camel, the feet of a deer, and the swiftness of the devil. It is a close relation of the Peruvian llama, which in turn is a cousin of the camel. The guanaco is envied for its soft reddish brown pelt. It is adept at craftily evading the hunter, but has little answer to the savagery of the winter, and large herds cluster together, hemmed in by the snow, and one by one they lie down in their clearings and die.

There are otters and coypu water-rats, and there are foxes four times the size of English ones, and whose liking for lambs and even full-grown sheep is just as strong. There is abundant bird life. The canoe Indians – the Yahgan – hunt almost all wildlife, but the now extinct foot Indians – the Ona – were even more eager in the chase. Apart from the sheep, and a little over a thousand cattle, the commonest domestic animal is the tough little *agua fresca* pony possibly descended from the Moorish ponies that went first to Spain, then across the seas to Chile. You may see a couple of these ponies, one bearing a *pasajero*, the other his luggage, followed by a pack of barking dogs, trotting across the hard

A shepherd of British stock rests in sight of part of the 20,000 sheep he helps to tend on the 40,000-acre de Bruyne family ranch.

Several—often quite separate
—racial strains compose the
people of Tierra del Fuego.
But the humbler numbers of
society are mostly part-Indian.

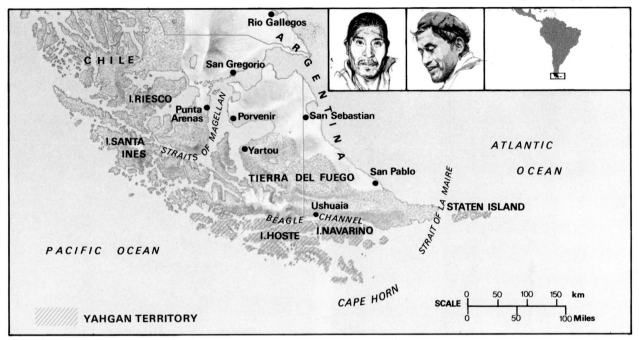

wastelands.

There are a few *pasajeros* still around. They are old bachelor farmhands who wander with their few possessions from job to job – that is, if there *are* any jobs. For a good four months of the year there are none – the daylight hours are too few. All there is to do is drink. The *pasajero* is most likely a Chilean or an Argentinean – the western two thirds of Tierra and its southernmost tip are Chilean, while the rest belongs to the Argentine – and he was perhaps initially lured southwards by the promise, almost always empty, of quick riches from gold and minerals. His symbol is the down-at-heel, tough, spurred gaucho boot. He is used to no kindness from nature; he knows what it is to be alone. Nature is an enemy. So are other men – especially if they are Indian.

Even Darwin was disgusted by the Fuegian Indians. Certainly no simple ranch-hand would be expected to take any more kindly to them. Disease and intertribal feuds were chiefly responsible for wiping out the Indians. But the white man, who arrived only at the end of the last century, accelerated the process.

Lucas Bridges was an exception. Almost all we know of the indigenous Indians is due to the work of him and his father, Thomas, who came in 1870 to the southernmost town in the world, Ushuaia, to spread the gospel. He was attracted by the challenge of taming such a wild country, and as he came to learn the ways of the Indian people, he found them attractive too. Thomas Bridges, the father, taught his sons to get on with the Yahgans, the canoe Indians who lived along the coast near Ushuaia, and he compiled a dictionary of Yahgan that ran to over 32,000 words. If the white man found the Yahgan a

fearsome people, the Yahgan found the inland Ona even more fearsome. It was the son Lucas Bridges who learnt to understand the Ona, now alas they have entirely died out.

In 1925 there were 150 Alcaluf Indians on Tierra del Fuego, mostly to the north and west. Today a few survive, some to be retrained as sailors in the Chilean navy. There were 40-50 Yahgan (see pages 120-123) of whom by 1966 only one aged woman remained, though there are a number of half-castes. The Aush, the eastern Ona, relations of the Ona proper, numbered merely three or four. They were probably the land's first occupants, and had been gradually pushed further and further towards the very tip of Tierra till they finally vanished. The Ona numbered almost 70 in 1925, just before two waves of measles destroyed over half of them.

The Ona were undoubtedly related to the Tehuelche of Patagonia, with whom they shared linguistic and physical features. The people of both tribes were hefty, stout but not fat—though many of them weighed 15 stone – and in stature often over six feet tall. They had long hair, but plucked their eyebrows and had almost no body hair nor beards: when a team of French scientists came in 1883 the Ona tried to pull their beards off, taking them for tobacco. A further factor that supports the theory that the Ona went south from Patagonia is their belief in a bird that does not exist on Tierra del Fuego, but whose description exactly fits that of the ostrich-like rhea of the Patagonian plains.

For an ignorant white man to meet the Ona would have been more alarming than a similar encounter with a Yahgan. The Ona language was harsh, guttural, ex- 113

People of Tierra del Fuego Chile and Argentina

Several thousand years ago her
ancestors crossed the Bering
Straits. Tierra del Fuego proved
the end of the line – in all senses.

plosive. They were huge. They were always armed. They went naked or wore a coat of reddish guanaco skin wrapped loosely round the shoulders. And though they certainly had a keen sense of humor, it was good manners among them to show no sign of emotion at meeting (and on various other occasions) – which could easily be construed among Europeans as unfriendliness, even hostility.

Respectful silence was the way to greet. When a hunter came home with the kill, the wife apparently ignored the results of the labor; only when the family set about eating the meat was it right to show glee. If, however, a hunting party had been out night and day, at great hardship a special, exceptional welcome might greet the hunters: those that had stayed at home would begin howling and barking like dogs. (The Ona were uncannily good mimics of all animals.) The returning hunters would reciprocate, and the whole scene of yelping and growling would be lit up by the heavy torches that the Ona carried at night. But on most occasions, modesty of expression and dignity were expected. Compliments were politely rebuffed – often with the expression 'You might annoy me', perhaps almost equiva-

Indian fires pricked the dark,
so passing mariners gave it the
name Tierra del Fuego — Land of
Fire. Now horses roam its bleak
and windswept plains.

115

Among the most southerly
permanent homes on earth, this
house, and its family of Spanish
and British stock, overlook
the icy channels.

lent to 'Don't flatter.'

The Ona also enjoyed the indirect approach. If a group of wrestling supporters wished to compliment the opposition on the performance of one of its wrestlers, the group's spokesman would say that its own team-mate was very fierce and strong – signifying that the opposing team's man had done well to resist him. They liked understatement too. At the end of a wrestling bout, submission was not bluntly admitted – the loser would leave his opponent with the words 'Sleepy am I.' Bad moods were not always detected through sour grunts and grumpy tones. The way the Ona painted their faces often showed how they felt. If they felt sullen, they augmented the face's expression by painting downward lines from the mouth and darkening the eye's hollow. If only some of our colleagues in the sophisticated world would give similar warning of their moods before we discover them!

The hardiness of the Ona was remarkable. The children often went naked even in winter. When the men fired their arrows, they too would always be naked, though most of the time they were clothed simply in three guanaco skins sewn together to make a loose-fitting cape held in place by the left hand which at the same time clutched the bow and the quiver that contained about

six arrows. They often wore a triangular headpiece, also of guanaco skin.

The guanaco was vital. From its sinews they made string for the bow. They made thongs from the tougher parts of the pelt. Out of the hock they made moccasins, which were stuffed with grass and worn fur out. They made cooking utensils and chippers out of the bones. They carried blood in the bladder and made a sort of blood sausage out of it. And of course the meat was the Ona staple diet.

They also caught and ate birds, which are plentiful among the islands. Sometimes, on a drizzly night, a man would be lowered from the cliff-top on the end of a seal-hide thong. He would then pounce on the nesting bird and, borrowing a technique from the Yahgan, would kill it with a bite in the neck. Or sometimes the women would be posted on the cliff-top, the men would wait below and a sudden lighting of torches on every side would so stun the birds that they would in panic dive from their perches and onto the ground below, where the Ona men would hold them down with their capes.

When wild game was scarce the Ona lived off tree-fungus (which also supplied tinder for their fires). Sometimes they collected the sap from the trees, but even a hungry person could enjoy but a little of it, as its taste

Bones of ships are strewn along
Magellan's Straits between
Patagonia and Tierra del Fuego
— this hulk drawn up as a
breakwater.

Where once the wild guanaco
— a kind of llama — used to
roam, sheep now graze on
Navarino Island, some of them
owned by the Chilean navy.

Ranchers no longer compete
with crafty Ona hunters (now
extinct) but the animals of this
icy, wet and stormy land face
many natural hazards.

117

People of Tierra del Fuego Chile and Argentina

Today's Fuegians use tough row-boats, but Yahgans once sailed flimsy canoes, usually paddled by women, and always with a fire burning astern.

Of all the world's capricious waters, those that lap these southern shores even today cast most terror into the hearts of hardened sailors.

was acrid and roughened both tongue and throat. If fungus was a poor man's dish, the greatest delicacy of all was whale. Sometimes a whale would be stranded ashore. Then the Ona would feast amid great rejoicing. If the whale were huge – which whales often are – the Ona had their own 'deep freeze' system: they would simply bury the beast under the ice-cold sand, and come back when the hungry season was upon them.

Ona men had one or several wives. Often a man would take an experienced, practical, middle-aged woman as first wife; later, a young, malleable second wife. In accordance with Ona good manners and reserve, a father would feign total lack of interest in a new baby, though secretly he was proud. The child's cradle was a ladder planted in the ground. The baby was strapped into it, and its eyes shaded from the snow's glare with a fox-skin eye-shield. If it cried, the mother would often quieten it by suddenly shrieking in its ear. To survive, a child had to be tough. The Ona had no enclosed houses at all – even in winter, they simply slept under a shelter of skins thrown across a straight row of stakes which leaned at 45 degrees and were placed to windward of the nearby fire.

There was no social organization. The Ona were undisciplined, and simply lived in small bands of friends and relations. If they quarreled, which they often did, they simply parted. As one Ona put it 'All the men are captains; all the women are sailors.' Vendettas often lasted for years and were a leading factor in the destruction of the tribe. Their arrows were often fired at each other, and they were very powerful. Bridges saw one that had entered a man's thigh as he bent down, and had come out again through the shoulder.

Many wives were captured in war; their new husbands had killed their old. The widows cut their hair in mourning – but in western terms, funeral and wedding bells were mixed. New wives were wise to obey husbands who – as the Ona put it – had 'blood in their eyes'. Captured wives were cosseted, but all wives had to bow before husbands. An angry husband might arrow a wife in the leg – and clumsy husbands were known to aim too high, fatally.

Vendettas would often continue for years. Camouflaged in white paint against the snow, or yellow against the grass, parties would ambush each other. The highly skilled tracking techniques of the Ona would be used to follow human enemies who were foolish enough to travel alone. On occasions camps were assailed, women and children slaughtered. Apart from a personal duel between two individual enemies, vendettas were ended only by wrestling matches or by the *jelj*, the tribal peace-ritual.

A wrestling match opened with speeches. Grievances were stated. Hoarse with emotion, but nevertheless in slow measured terms, each side called the other 'fox-like' or 'dog-like'. Now and then a bereaved mother might break into a howl of woe.

The wrestling started when a man leapt forward with

Desolate Navarino Island has only a handful of permanent inhabitants — among them this elderly English shepherd and a half-caste English boy.

left hand outstretched, which would be clasped by an opponent's right hand. The fighters would clinch, remaining if possible in a fully upright position. They would take turns to fight, till all the members of one side were too tired and battered to go on. Unwritten rules forbade scratching, or attacks on eyes or ears. A breach of such rules would be derided with cries of 'Is it a dog?'

The *jelj* was a weightier truce. Each member painted with red and white spots, the parties would approach and sit silently opposite each other for many long minutes. Then each man would choose one of his enemies. Dodging and running the enemy would come nearer and nearer his opposite number, who would fire five disc-tipped arrows at him till the range was point blank. Then the process was reversed. The *jelj* marked an end to tribal conflict – for a while.

Ritual, whether part of a peace ceremony or accompanying the initiation of a boy into adulthood, was mainly for men. They enjoyed ritual occasions, which often went together with rollicking laughter, especially when men, dressed up as dreaded supernatural figures, came out of the large ceremonial wigwam and terrorized the women. But there were dances which the women could happily watch – the caterpillar dance, when the men, painted in red and white horizontal lines, linked up one behind the other and jigged in a chain forward and sideways; or the frog dance, when the men covered in ash leapt between the shelters; or better still for the women, the push-me-down dance, when the men feigned cripple and allowed the women to 'knock them down dead', recalling the days when the women were superior to men.

Real death was accompanied with self-inflicted wounds on the mourners, who dismantled the shelter and burned the bow and arrows of the dead man – sometimes before he had actually died. But soon after the white men came death among the Ona easily outnumbered births. They had no answer to diseases they were not accustomed to.

The ruthless expansion of ranches in the north, just south of the Magellan Straits, was countered in 1893 with a gold rush along the Beagle Channel towards the south. The prospectors found little gold, but brought the rifle, the gin-bottle and diseases. Punta Arenas is still today a disorderly shanty town, relic of that first frantic rush. But the newcomers varied, from the Salesian priests and the Bridges family, to navvies from the Dalmatian coast (now part of Yugoslavia) who were the most numerous early arrivals. In later years Italians came most frequently. British and German ranchers braved the wilds. There were all types of adventurer, an Austrian miner, a Danish concertina-player, even an 18-strong family of Sikhs from India who now live in Punta Arenas. Near Ushuaia there is a Basque who has a half-Yahgan wife. There are Chilotes working along the Beagle Channel – products of the union between Spanish soldiers and Chono, Mapuche and Araucano women from the island of Chiloé off the Chilean coast. The few surviving descendants of the people who were once lords of the land are almost all intermingled with the diverse people who came to Tierra del Fuego in the last hundred years.

There are families – one rancher has a hundred descendants – but there are no communities with any identity unique to the land. The people who went to Tierra del Fuego, like the Ona before them, are essentially loners. The common factor that unites them is the struggle against hostile elements. Outsiders like men from the oil companies come and go. (Chile's only oil has recently been discovered in Tierra.) Even tourists sometimes come to see the world's southernmost town.

The Indians have become much, much fewer. The white man is barely more prolific than he was fifty years ago. There are 3,000 sheep to every human on Tierra del Fuego. There are fewer smoke fires than when Magellan first saw them and took their name for his new-found land. But the land remains as it was, gale-swept and bare. Ranches and missions have become well established, but the elements remain in control.

The last of the Yahgan
Chile and Argentina

For the Asiatic peoples who crossed the Bering Straits, many thousands of years ago, and then swarmed down to populate the Americas, Tierra del Fuego was the end of the road. Today it is truly the end of the road for those who went furthest of all, the Yahgan Indians, the most southerly dwellers in this most southerly of permanently inhabited lands. Today few, if any, Yahgan Indians survive – possibly one old woman at the time of writing. It is apt, therefore, to speak of the Yahgan in the past tense.

Tierra del Fuego, separated from the South American mainland by the Magellan Straits, belongs partly to Argentina and partly to Chile: it consists of one large island and a great many smaller islands. In 1826 a British ship, *HMS Beagle*, was sent to survey the region, and gave its name to a narrow channel that lay south of that largest island. It was here, along the rocky shores of Beagle Channel and on the islands to the south, that the Yahgan Indians, who called themselves Yamoma, had their homeland. To the north, the east and the west lived their neighbors, the Ona, the Aush or Eastern Ona and the Alacaluf: the Yahgan, living in even less hospitable country, appeared even more primitive than these to the newcomers and at once aroused interest as possible candidates for Christianity and civilization. A few of them were taken back to England in the *Beagle*, taught the Gospel and various crafts, given ridiculous names like York Minster, Jimmy Button and Fuegia Basket, and even presented to King William IV and Queen Adelaide. Two years later the *Beagle* bore them home again. This time Charles Darwin was on board.

It was a voyage of scientific importance, for Darwin was making some of the observations that led eventually to *The Origin of Species*. When he saw them in their own country, Darwin took a poor view of the Yahgan. The poverty and filth in which they lived led him to question their full membership of the human race, and perhaps to entertain for the first time the notion of the missing link.

The Yahgan were short: they were often under five feet tall and most just topped five feet. They were dwarfs compared to their large neighbors, the Ona. Their stunted height may derive from endless crouching in canoes; it is an advantage to be small in a flimsy craft bobbing awkwardly in unpleasant waters. They were also extremely strong, with broad shoulders: white men learned that they would be severely battered if they tried to wrestle with a Yahgan.

Their huts were simple. They were scattered, half-buried wigwam hovels, made of branches, and roofed with turf and grass. They smelt strongly – of smoke, decomposed whale-blubber and years of refuse flung in heaps outside. The rubbish, casually chucked out of the wigwams, made natural horse-shoe shaped walls around them. Often and incongruously, beautiful wild flowers and currants would overgrow these mounds. And from the old bones, shells and rubbish that they have found on these piles, archaeologists have best been able to date the Yahgan's arrival on Tierra del Fuego. They have probably been there over 2,000 years.

Soon after the second voyage of the *Beagle*, an Anglican mission was established at Ushuaia ('inner harbor to the westward') – and heroically developed over the years. With the mission came Thomas Bridges, a tough but sensitive clergyman, who was the first to study the life of the Yahgan, and to realize that Darwin may have been misled in his disparaging judgement of them.

Thomas Bridges compiled a dictionary of the Yahgan language, which ran to 32,000 words: there were few words to express abstract ideas, and the numerals were very limited in range. They only had words for one, two and three: four was 'twice two,' five was 'one hand,' and so on. But there were words enough for matters concerned with their way of life; there were five words for snow, for example, and seven for beach or shore, and many fine shades of meaning could be simply expressed. Where we would use a rambling sentence, they had succinct words. There was one word for the idea 'to come upon a hard substance when biting into something soft,' for instance, when you bite into a mussel and find a pearl.

The Yahgan's culture and life-style were in harmony with their environment. And their environment was a particularly harsh one: perhaps the most remarkable characteristic of the tribe was their physical hardihood. Their bodies were covered in rolls of fat, for warmth and as a store of energy, on the same principle as the Bushmen of South Africa, who also have to survive for long periods without food. In this bitterly cold land they went practically naked, wearing nothing but a tiny apron for modesty and occasionally an inadequate cloak made from the skins of the fox or the sea otter. Their exposure was less from choice than from necessity. There were certainly not enough fox or otter skins to go round. The hides of hair-seal were usually eaten or cut into thongs used for lowering audacious bird-hunters over cliff-tops. Their Ona neighbors kept warm in the skins of the guanaco (a kind of llama), but this useful animal was scarce where the Yahgan lived. Their word for a poor person was 'body only' – and many of them, especially the young men, qualified for the epithet. Sometimes the only protection they had against the wind and the snow was a layer of grease.

Yahgan women were as tough as their men. In the icy waters around Tierra del Fuego, the women would swim and dive for the shellfish, which with fish, seals, birds and berries, made up the Yahgan's diet. It was the women who paddled the canoes, and navigated the difficult rocky coastline. The canoes were originally flimsy, leaky structures made of bark, but at some point the Yahgan learned to make dug-out canoes which were a good deal safer, though less speedy and manoeuvrable. The Yahgan

120

She is the last surviving member of her tribe, the Yahgan of Patagonia, once 3,000 strong but destroyed by diseases and despair.

Yahgan Chile and Argentina

This old man of mixed blood
is the official chief of the
Yahgan, a tribe which
exists no more. His wife is
part-Ona, also sadly reduced.

were entirely dependent on their boats for their subsistence and their transport: they were very much a
coastal people and there was little to attract them inland.
They were mortally afraid of the Ona, and also of
various supernatural presences they believed to inhabit
the hinterland.

The Yahgan understandably placed a high value on fire.
They used firestone or iron pyrites as their source of fire,
digging it from one particular source on the borders of
their own territory and that of the Alacaluf. The quantity
of waste there shows that the site has been worked for
centuries. From the firestone, the Yahgan would strike
sparks to ignite a kind of fungus which was kept dry in
the bladder of a seal or guanaco and served excellently
as tinder. In practice, they would keep fires going continually and seldom needed to relight them: they even
carried fires to sea with them, burning on little piles of
sand or turf in their canoes. There was little danger of
setting their sodden craft alight.

They also used fires to send smoke-signals, especially
at times of alarm and danger: it was apparently the
sight of these smoke-columns, rising at intervals for
miles along the coast – and prompted by their own
arrival – which suggested to Magellan the first name that
he gave the land: 'Land of Smoke.' Charles V of Spain
changed it to Land of Fire, since he thought it a nicer
name for his new acquisition, adding that there was, of
course, no smoke without fire. Yet neither name may
seem wholly apt for this very un-fiery country. Perhaps
with the discovery of oil and the new orange flame that
sometimes glows in the sky, the old name may become
more suitable.

The technology of the Yahgan was limited, and, like
their language and physique, specifically adapted to
their environment. For drinking-vessels they used large
sea-shells; for arrow-heads and knives, they used flint
or agate. Their huts were crude. But their food-gathering
techniques were well developed. They had slings for
hunting, and could bring down their prey with stones
thrown hard and accurately by hand. They used bows
and arrows as well, but their principal weapon was the
spear. They would spear fish and birds, and they had a
special four-pronged implement for dislodging mussels
and limpets from the rocks; for catching seals, porpoises,
and even small whales, they had a fairly sophisticated
method of harpooning. For catching the loggerhead or
steamer duck – an enormous bird, weighing up to 20
pounds – they used a fine noose, manipulated by a man
in hiding; they caught the cormorant or shag with baited
and barbed lines, and they had an elaborate technique
for netting fish in estuaries.

Darwin had assumed that the Yahgan were cannibals:
they were not. When they were at their wits' end for food
they would eat animal hides and even their own guanaco
skin moccasins. They did practise *tabacana*, the strang-
ling of the aged and hopelessly sick. While they had

virtually no religion, they had legends and folklore, and a definite ethical code. For example they disapproved more of homicide than did the Ona.

They had no god either good or bad, but they had several supernatural enemies to beware of, apart from their all-too-real Ona neighbors. There were the mythical and feared wild-men-in-the-woods whose heads had bald patches from being rubbed against the trees. And there were ghosts, especially those of drowned colleagues. For them, the Yahgan would sometimes light a shore-side fire, and wait patiently at night for the ghosts to come up out of the sea for a bit of warmth. And there were *lakooma* who haunted lakes and bays. Whirlpools and strong springs which came up from lake beds and melted the ice in winter were attributed to the movements of *lakooma*.

The Yahgan were a loosely-organized people, with little defined social structure, and perhaps for this reason, they were quarrelsome and prone to vendetta. Recently the surviving remnant of the tribe has had a 'chief', a title alien to the people; but he is a half-caste. For the true Yahgan Indians have all but died out.

Though the Yahgan learned to cope with the adverse conditions in which they had lived for so many centuries, they had no defence against contact with Europeans and their unfamiliar diseases – measles in particular. And progressively their country was opened up. The Argentinian and Chilean governments started to exercise their authority. Extensive sheep farming began to be developed; gold was discovered, and, more recently, oil. Today Ushuaia has progressed from a handful of wooden huts into an important air and naval base.

Alongside these changes Yahgan society has dwindled. There were about three thousand of them when Darwin came, but only 170 by 1908; in 1932 there were 43 survivors, including some half-castes. And at the time of writing the ancient Yahgan people are represented by precisely one old lady, one survivor to carry the whole of their memory, their identity.

It was a long road that brought them from the plains of Asia to the stormy desolation of the Land of Fire; and they have reached the end of it.

From a distance of half a century or more, it is instructive, even chastening, to note the injustice of the deductions that even professional anthropological commentators brought to their descriptions of the less civilized, building the prejudices that Western man has long nurtured. A H Keane, President of the Royal Anthropological Society, writing in 1908 on the Yahgan and their neighbors, in *The World's Peoples*:

'Now and then a whale is stranded on the coast, and then there is a great gorge, after which the remains of the feast are buried in a big hole and the place is then forgotten, which shows an intelligence almost inferior to that of a

The impact of a vigorous alien culture alone was enough to dissolve the hope of the three southernmost tribes on earth.

This boy's Yahgan ancestors were credited with 'less intelligence than dogs.' Yet his lost language contained 52,000 words.

dog, who never forgets his bone .... Owing to rigid climate and bad treatment, the mortality of children under ten years is excessive. The mother's love lasts until the child is weaned, and is completely gone when the child is seven or eight years old. The Fuegians' only lasting love is the love of self. As there are no real family ties, the word "authority" is devoid of meaning, and the head of the family group is simply an autocrat who does what he likes with its members – throws them overboard, for instance to lighten the boat in a storm.'

Welsh of Patagonia
Argentina

During their great years of overseas expansion, the British established themselves in many quarters of the globe, and not only in the countries which became part of their extensive but short-lived Empire. Today there are a number of colonies large and small, of people who are British by origin but now live under various foreign flags. At one extreme, there is the tiny, impoverished English community who live on the Caribbean island of Utila under the flag of the Republic of Honduras; at the other, there is in Argentina one of the largest, most prosperous groups of British expatriates outside the British Commonwealth. Not all are Englishmen: many are Scots and Welsh, with curious histories of emigration behind them. And among these stories, perhaps the most remarkable is that of the Welshmen of Patagonia.

In Wales, during the middle years of the 19th century, the spread of popular education and increase in literacy encouraged nationalistic sentiment to develop. There was a great deal of unemployment and poverty in their small, overshadowed country and Welshmen began to feel with some vehemence that they were being exploited by the English. Over and above their economic considerations, there were suspicions that the very identity, the Welshness of Wales, was seriously threatened.

In the 1850s an increasing number of Welshmen believed that emigration was the only answer, and the Welsh Emigration Society was established to look into possibilities. The United States was thought at first to be the obvious place for settlement. But it was soon decided, possibly unjustifiably, that in that great 'melting pot,' a small group of Welsh immigrants might lose its identity and become assimilated into a uniform Americanism. Other countries – Australia, New Zealand, British Columbia – were considered with a view to establishing a self-governing Welsh colony. But in none of these countries could the autonomy of such a colony be guaranteed.

It was about this time that the Argentinian government, anxious to open up the interior of its country to develop a high-grade cattle industry, found that one of its problems was a shortage of labor. 'To govern,' said Juan Bautista Alberdi, an influential Argentinian publicist, 'is to populate'; and so a welcome was extended to many groups of potential immigrants, particularly the Welsh Emigration Society. In the south, in the territory loosely called Patagonia, there was plenty of space for them.

'Patagonia' refers sometimes to the whole South America south of the 39th parallel, including part of Chile, but more usually to the Argentinian plateau from that latitude down to the islands of Cape Horn and including Tierra del Fuego. In this arid land where the cold Falkland Current and the rain-shadow of the Andes limit rainfall, and where the vegetation is mostly low brush and clumps of bunch grasses with a rare tree here and there, the Welsh happily set up their colony. Dry

24

12

In 1865 a shipload of Welsh
men and women sailed for
far Patagonia; though
Argentines now, many still
speak Welsh — and sing it.

Welsh of Patagonia Argentina

The Welsh pioneers came to a
land peopled by only a few
Indians. But they mastered
the pampas, and now they are
expert sheep ranchers.

Wool brings a steady income today. But until a Mrs Aaron Jenkins found irrigation the key to wheat-growing, early survival was precarious.

cold winds sweep fiercely over that inhospitable flat table-land and the cliffs of the coastal region. It was, nevertheless, a satisfactory arrangement on both sides. The Argentinians would be helped in the development of their country; and the Welsh were in turn guaranteed the isolation and autonomy they desired. After a preliminary survey by John Jones and Sir Love Jones Parry Madryn, which reported favorably in spite of the desolation, the Argentinian government promised grants of land, and practical support in the form of sheep and horses and grain.

The enterprise was put in hand. In May 1865, the *Mimosa* sailed from Liverpool, flying the Red Dragon of Wales, and the emigrants, who crowded the decks and sang hymns at the time of departure, numbered only 153 out of the five hundred chosen prospective emigrants.

It was a difficult voyage. The *Mimosa,* a tea-clipper of 450 tons, was crudely adapted to carry passengers: the hold was divided up into cabins by rough planking, and there were no portholes. For the two-month voyage and for the rough food provided on board, each emigrant had paid £12.

Morale was high. It needed to be: an arduous future lay before the colonists. They were to establish and feed themselves on a wholly uncultivated coast, but only four of them had any farming experience, most of the men being miners and quarry-workers; and in this rough dangerous country, a bone-setter named John Williams was the nearest they had to a doctor. They landed in July on the beach at Golfo Nuevo, a fine natural harbor some three hundred miles south of Buenos Aires which was separated by more than forty miles of arid desert from the Chubut valley in which they intended to settle. On the very first day they suffered their first casualty, a young man called David Williams, perhaps slightly crazed by the voyage and the landing, ran off wildly in search of the Chubut. His bones were found years later.

They stayed three weeks at their point of landing, which they named Port Madryn after Sir Love Jones Parry Madryn, and sheltered in caves from the parching gales at Patagonia. Then they embarked on the long walk to the valley of the river Chubut with only a wheelbarrow for wheeled transport.

When they reached the valley they named it in Welsh, 'Camwy' or 'winding valley'. They named their first settlement of dug-out shelters Tre Rawson, or Rawson town, after the Argentinian Minister of the Interior who had sponsored their arrival. But there was nothing of the Welsh greenness and fertility to Camwy as they found it: there was only an expanse of dry yellow sand, with just a few red willows and a few clumps of pampas grass along the riverside.

In these unpromising surroundings and with no experience to guide them, they tried to grow wheat from seed which they had brought with them. But there was not enough rain, and their clumsy efforts failed com-

Welshness is now diluted. Señora Olwyn Jones drinks traditional green Argentinian *yerba* tea in the *mate* gourd.

129

This couple are off to Sunday
chapel and a rousing Welsh
sermon. But most Welsh
descendants speak better
Spanish; many are Catholic.

pletely. The colonists would probably have starved had
not the Argentinian government, prompted by Dr
Rawson, kept its promise and supplied them for three
years with cattle, sheep, horses and grain. Even with this
help, supplemented from time to time when British
warships called with supplies, many of the colonists were
so disheartened that they left the colony for other more
promising regions of Argentina.

Then, in 1868, when the colony was reduced to about
ninety people, an epoch-making discovery was made.
According to tradition, a farmer called Aaron Jenkins,
in despair at the parched conditions of his wheat, tried
out his wife's suggestion that he should water his land
by digging a ditch from the river. The result was startling
and spectacular. From then on wherever this irrigation
technique was used, the sterile land blossomed and produced wheat of such quality that it was fetching top
prices in the Buenos Aires market within seven years.

Then it turned out that another problem, which had
caused anxiety at the beginning, was not a problem after
all. The Tehuelche Indians of the country were not
hostile, as had been feared. On the contrary, they became
the colonists' best friends. They taught the Welshmen
how to break and manage horses, how to use the *bolas*
and the lasso, and how to hunt the guanaco (a species of
llama) and the rhea (a kind of ostrich) for food. Friend-
ship and trade developed between the two peoples. In

return for the Indians' kindness, the colonists refused to
take part in the so-called War of the Desert in 1879-83,
in fact a campaign of simple extermination, largely responsible for the fact that Argentina now has practically
no Indian population at all. The campaign gained the
Presidency of the country for its leader, General Julio
A Roca, who closed his ears to the Welsh colonists'
appeals on behalf of the Indians.

By their intervention, albeit ineffectual, the colonists
were not simply displaying good nature and gratitude:
they had come to the Chubut valley for its remoteness,
they did not want it to be opened up and developed on
the lines to which the Argentinian government was by
now committed.

They were satisfied with things as they were. The work
of irrigation was under way and the Chubut valley had
started to change from a desert into the narrow but rich
strip of farming country that it is today. They built new,
more permanent houses, imported agricultural mach-
inery, and acquired a ship to carry their produce to
Buenos Aires. The stream of desertions not only stopped;
it was reversed. News of this prosperity went back to
Wales, from which more and more people came; in 1880
the colony numbered some 800 people. In 1881 the town
of Trelew was established and named after Lewis Jones,
one of the most famous of the early settlers, who died in
1903. In 1885 some of the colonists moved inland and

settled at Sarmiento and Esquel among the foothills of the Andes. Soon afterwards a light railway was established, linking Puerto Madryn (as Port Madryn is now called) with the Chubut valley. Sheep-farming grew rapidly, as elsewhere in Patagonia and throughout Argentina, and wool began to compete with agrarian produce.

This prosperous development was inevitably achieved at the cost of the isolation and independence for which the Welsh had originally come to Argentina. For a time, their autonomy was maintained. The early colonists appointed their own governor, elected a legislature of twelve, instituted trial by jury; they opened chapels and schools, published their own newspapers, held their own *eisteddfod*.

But they were living under Argentinian flag and had accepted Argentinian citizenship, and the implications of this were bound to come home to them sooner or later. In 1875 an Argentinian police chief arrived among them to exercise powers that were ill-defined but appeared to be extensive. Nine years later the Chubut valley was formally declared a Territory of the Argentine Republic, and in Tre Rawson – now called simply Rawson – an Argentinian governor was installed. Thenceforward the colony came under much closer control from Buenos Aires, which endangered its Welsh character. The authorities insisted that Spanish should be taught in schools and encouraged immigration of other people notably Italians. The colonists were also obliged to undertake military training. To the outrage of their nonconformist consciences it was decided that Sunday should be the day for parades. The rebellious passions that were engendered were only soothed when President Roca made a visit in person and excused the Welshmen from so violating their Sabbath.

Yet the original Pilgrim Fathers of this Welsh colony would be grieved if they saw how far their cause has been lost in Patagonia today. Welshness remains, but it is diluted and threatened: the Welsh language is indeed spoken, but mostly by the older generation, and it is no longer taught in the schools. The leadership of the community is more and more passing from the Welsh to Argentinians of Spanish or Italian origin; and the fifty-acre allotments of land, which must have seemed enormous to the first colonists when they arrived from their mining towns and quarry-villages, have tied their descendants down to subsistence farming, whereas later immigrants were able to plan on a larger scale. The community is, in fact, definitely poor and decreasingly Welsh: there has been much intermarriage, and this has often led to what the Founding Fathers would have regarded as the worst treachery of all, an abandonment of the severely Calvinistic religion and the bare chapels of Wales, and an assimilation of the Roman Catholic religious influences of Argentina.

But the colony continues to be recognizably Welsh.

In 1965 the colonists celebrated the centenary of their arrival in the country, with festivities generously subsidized by the Argentinian government. Trelaw is moderately prosperous, but Puerto Madryn is something of a ghost town. A changing economy has reduced its old importance as a center of the region's trade. In Rawson, in Madryn, in Trelaw, in the large village of Gaiman, the visitor who is invited into some private house or chapel may suppose himself to be seven thousand miles away in Wales: the names of the people, their talent and passion for song, their social patterns, their language, their white slate-roofed cottages, their flowery gardens and their heavily loaded tea-tables contribute to the illusion. He may hear it claimed that in this loose community of some five thousand people, there are more speakers of the Welsh language than can now be found at home in Wales.

The process of assimilation is far from complete; and when – among these loyal Argentinians who mostly speak Spanish – you hear pure Celtic voices singing *Land of our Fathers* once again, you know that you are encountering something more than a nostalgic memory, a lost dream.

129

In the town of Gaiman, 7,000 miles from Wales, Williams 'The Shop' sells groceries and regrets the thinning of Welsh culture.

Glossary to the peoples of highland South America

The people who live in highland South America tend either to be Spanish, *mestizo* or Indian. For over 400 years the Spanish have lived in South America and although in a minority, have influenced every aspect of life: in religion, language, culture and technology. In the Andean countries the Spanish play a leading role in politics and business and tend to own big estates, or *haciendas,* although these are neither as many nor as large (with rare exceptions) as they were a couple of hundred years ago. The official language in all Andean countries is Spanish. Religion is officially Roman Catholic. In winter Spanish matadors travel to the high Andean capitals to fight bulls. The enormous mineral wealth of the Andes has been developed largely by the Spanish: gold, silver, copper, platinum, iron ore, nitrates, petroleum products and zinc all boost the economies of these countries.

Despite the richness of the Spanish heritage the Andean region is by no means a second Spain. The Spaniards are in fact numerically small. And since the first days of the Conquest they have taken Indian wives and mistresses with the result that today the large majority of the Latin American population are *mestizos,* people of mixed Spanish-Indian blood. In the *mestizos* is mingled the fire of the Spaniards and the tenacity and craftsmanship of the Andean Indian. Except in Chile, where people of European origin overwhelmingly predominate, *mestizos* have risen in all spheres of political and economic life. In the northern Andean countries, Colombia and Venezuela, there are a few mulattos (mixed negroes and whites) and some full-blood negroes.

As well as the Spanish minority there are a few other small groups of Europeans in the Andean region. Most remarkable is the group of Welsh farmers in Patagonia. They settled there during the last century when the land was too poor for even the local people to gain a livelihood. By means of careful irrigation they made the land wonderfully productive. The waves of immigration from Europe during the political upheavals of last century also brought a handful of Germans to Chile. Today they are a thriving community around Valdivia. German Jews found refuge in Chile, Bolivia and Peru during the 1930s, and – ironically – Nazi refugees followed in the late 1940s. English and Scottish families have been settled in this area since the late 19th century, coming in as contractors for railway building, in the electrical industry and as manufacturers – particularly in Chile, when the English also developed the nitrate industry. Very far south in Tierra del Fuego a few hardy British sheep farmers are scattered. US-owned companies developed copper mining in Chile, and attracted some Americans up to nationalization in the 1970s. On the coast of Peru there are physical traces of Chinese immigration surviving from last century when Chinese went to work on sugar plantations and to dig guano.

In the Andes are found the most thriving and numerous Indian communities of South America. This great mountain chain over 5,000 miles long stretching from the Caribbean coast of Venezuela to the Straits of Magellan is a unique feature of the world: a geographical, climatic and cultural barrier that is also a refuge. There are still only three railway lines running latitudinally across the Andes. The culture of the Andean Indians is and has always been radically different from that of the tropical forest tribes. It is more sophisticated in every way, which is perhaps the reason these people have survived in the face of foreign intrusions. The greatest destruction of the South American Indians was along the coasts and the rivers, where the Europeans, water-borne and maintaining contact with their homelands, came with overwhelming force to get rubber, diamonds and gold. Any Indians who offered resistance were ruthlessly murdered. But the Central Andes were well beyond the bounds of ordinary migration – even today travel in the Andes is difficult, and the high altitude puts a strain on European lungs. There are probably more Indians today in the Andes than at the time of the Conquest.

The main Indian settlements are in Bolivia where 70 per cent of the population is Indian, in Peru where it is 46 per cent, and in Ecuador where it is 30 per cent. In the northern and southern extremities of the Andes there are only a few American Indians left. The once mighty Araucanian tribe of Chile is now confined to land between the Bio-Bio and Tolten rivers south of Concepción, and comprises less than 5 per cent of the population. In Colombia and Venezuela less than 5 per cent are Indians.

A century or two before the Spanish Conquest, before the spread of the Inca empire, there were a hundred small states and kingdoms in the Andes. At its height the Inca Empire stretched from the south of Colombia to central Chile – a distance greater than the width of the entire USA or across Europe from the Atlantic to the Caspian Sea. The only central Andean people to escape Inca subjugation were people like the Campa who lived in the buttress ranges of the Andes which run at right angles to the main range and stretch into the Amazonian plain.

The Inca Background

Spanish domination superseded one of the most remarkable territorial empires the world has known. The Indians of the central Andean massif have never recovered from the immense shock of the destruction of the culture and their power. Today's fragments of the Indian community formerly under Inca rule all suffer from what, to them, is an obscure loss of cohesion and *raison d'être.*

Life under Inca rule was hard but stable. Commoners had to give two-thirds of their produce to the state. They had to join the armies, build the public buildings, provide the Inca and the nobility with domestic servants, mistresses and concubines. They would give them pretty

South America's racial web is the most intricate in the world, and it varies country by country. This chart helps you to unravel it.

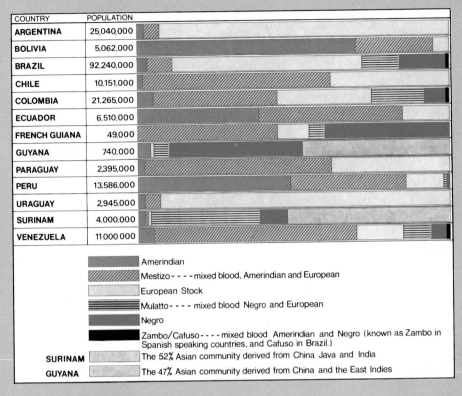

COUNTRY	POPULATION
ARGENTINA	25,040,000
BOLIVIA	5,062,000
BRAZIL	92,240,000
CHILE	10,151,000
COLOMBIA	21,265,000
ECUADOR	6,510,000
FRENCH GUIANA	49,000
GUYANA	740,000
PARAGUAY	2,395,000
PERU	13,586,000
URAGUAY	2,945,000
SURINAM	4,000,000
VENEZUELA	11 000 000

Amerindian

Mestizo - - - - mixed blood, Amerindian and European

European Stock

Mulatto - - - - mixed blood Negro and European

Negro

Zambo/Cafuso - - - - mixed blood Amerindian and Negro (known as Zambo in Spanish speaking countries, and Cafuso in Brazil.)

SURINAM — The 52% Asian community derived from China Java and India

GUYANA — The 47% Asian community derived from China and the East Indies

girls as 'chosen women'. If they were exceptionally beautiful they might be awarded the privilege of joining the Inca's retinue of women. Any soldier who ever showed fear was punished by death.

It was a rich society, founded on the ability to produce a surplus of crops. The high-sided valleys were covered with productive terraces. Guano was carried on the backs of llamas up from the coast for fertilizing the fields. At least thirty species of crops were grown, each with many different varieties. The variety of potatoes alone was enormous. It was this highly efficient farming which allowed for stratification in Inca society. Each family could produce more than they wanted for subsistence, which released men for other more specialized occupations. There were many goldsmiths, weavers, and administrators.

To be a noble one had either to be chief of a vassal state or to be born of a noble's family which claimed descent from an Inca. There was no system of hereditary succession: the Inca himself could be anyone of Inca descent who was judged to have the qualities of a ruler. There was much jostling of status between nobles, for some claimed closer relationship to the Inca than others. The Incas themselves – that is to say, the rulers of the people who came to be known by the same name as their rulers – were believed divine. In the later days of the Empire they were so exclusive that they could not marry any but their full-blooded sister but would be accompanied by a retinue of concubines and mistresses. The

priests were also ranked in a hierarchy. There were colleges where girls were sent to lead a spiritual life. Many stayed chaste all their lives in the service of the Sun God. The cities were populous by any standard of the time. Cuzco had 100,000 inhabitants when it was conquered in 1634. The buildings of the towns were beautifully conceived. Streets were laid out in straight lines. There were religious and administrative buildings. There was also a great quantity of gold, emeralds, silver and all the symbols of wealth for which the Europeans craved in the age of discovery. Yet despite the sophistication of the Incas they had no writing nor any form of written records – possibly, it is suggested, deliberately, to retain the oral secrecy of the hereditary élite.

Various peoples today claim descent from the people known as the Incas. But with the élite gone, the culture swiftly lost its confidence and sense of unity. Today's Quechua, who speak the Inca language, are peasant farmers; and although the Central Andes is still rich in culture, it is deeply penetrated by Spanish influences. Many are Roman Catholics, many speak Spanish and many have adapted themselves to a modern economy, like the Otavalo who are famous as merchants and weavers. Only a few groups – and not those formerly within the circle of Inca power – live as they have for hundreds of years with little outside influence, like the Chipaya. Many groups have also died out completely, like the Pantangoro, or become indistinguishable from surrounding peoples, like the Esmeraldas.

ABURRA *Population:* unknown. Language group: Choco. Once found in Colombia in the province of Aburra between the Madalena and Cauca Rivers, the Aburra group of tribes are now all feared extinct or integrated into other groups. In the 16th century when they first came in contact with the Spanish, partly out of fear and partly for religious reasons, many Aburra tribes committed mass suicide. Early chroniclers recorded that Aburra people kept mute dogs. They subsisted by cultivating maize, beans, manioc, yams and sweet potatoes and by hunting. The most sought-after game were peccaries. Whilst several tribes around them used bows and arrows for hunting, the Aburra tribes instead used spears. They built large houses and were famous for their construction of aqueducts and broad roads. Though they were warlike people they neither sacrificed nor ate their prisoners as did some of the neighboring tribes. Their clothes were made of large blankets with which they wore feather headdresses; and they painted themselves for decoration.

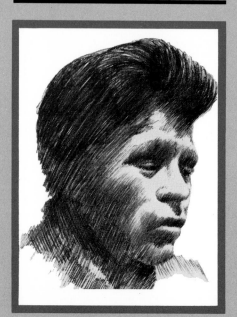

ALACALUF *Population:* 200. Language group: Alacaluf. Often called the 'canoe Indians,' the Alacaluf live on the archipelago from the Gulf of Peras to the islands west of Tierra del Fuego along the coast of Chile. They rely heavily on the sea and boats as their land has only sparse vegetation, and is often snow-covered and impossible to cross. In the past there were many small bands of Alacaluf; 20 years ago only about 200 individuals survived; reports in recent years indicate that their numbers are now increasing. Only a few manage to preserve their traditional way of life. They live in small family bands eating mostly fish and shell-fish and sometimes stranded whales or sea lions. They rarely grow crops, but gather some wild vegetables, hunt otters and caypus with the help of dogs, and eat birds. Because of the great humidity – over 120 inches of rain each year – it is almost impossible to store food, and food has to be found daily. Their huts, occupied by a single family, are oval and built on a framework of poles stuck firmly into the ground. Their most noteworthy craft is basketry. There is no marriage ceremony; the man simply moves in with his woman's family and while there are no pre-marital sexual restrictions, husbands become jealous and beat their wives on suspicion of infidelity.

AMANI (see PANTANGORO)

ARAUCANIANS *Population:* 300,000. Language group: Araucanian. Before the Spanish Conquest the Auracanian tribes covered vast areas in Chile. They fiercely resisted the Spanish for many years, destroying Santiago a year after Valdivia founded it in 1541, and, in 1554, under Lautaro, his former groom and foster son, defeating and killing Valdivia at Tucapa. Today most of them live between the Bio-Bio river and the Canal of Chacao. Only a few survive east of the Andes on the pampas. The best known tribes are the Picunche, the Mapuche and the Huilliche of which the Mapuche are the largest and most independent surviving group. Although for over 300 years the Mapuche have resisted the Chileans' attempts to westernize them, contact in both war and peace has resulted in many changes. They now live on reservations where they grow wheat, potatoes and other cultivated crops. They also herd sheep, cattle and horses, all of which were introduced by the Chileans. The homestead houses a man and his wife, his parents and his children, and also sometimes his brothers and sisters. Marriage takes place after a long courtship, often only after the girl is pregnant. A man normally marries a kinswoman from his mother's side – a wife from his father's side is prohibited – and pays a bride-price for her. The chief rules over both villages and reservations. Christianity has only gradually superseded the traditional beliefs. The Araucanians have many gods and powerful shamans. Central to Mapuche religion are

ancestral spirits. Ancestors can return to earth, but are only likely to do so if their descendants have been failing in their ritual duties. Should the spirit return, there is also great danger to him from the earthly forces of evil. The Mapuche fear a return of spirits of the dead, not only for what might happen to the spirits, but also for what might happen to their surviving descendants.

ARHUACO. The Arhuaco are a group of tribes—Ica, Saha, Kogi (Cagaba) and Bintigwa—of which the Kogi (q.v.) are the most important.

ATACAMA *Population:* 1,000. Language group: Kunza. The Atacama have mostly been absorbed by the Aymara (*q.v.*) and *mestizos* (*q.v.*) of Peru and Bolivia. Only a few live the traditional life in the Puma de Jujuy and in isolated parts of the Upper Rio Con Basin. They lived in the desert where they herded llamas and alpacas, scratching a precarious living from the soil. Their houses were often fortified—as were their villages— and solidly built of stone. Their weapons included bows and arrows, slings and wooden knuckle dusters and they made protective armor of cloth or leather. They grew maize as a staple food and hunted and fished. As farming was precarious they built granaries in caves and dried foods like fish. They were heavily dependent on their trading activities and exchanged llama hair blankets and ropes for many of the necessities they could not produce themselves, and for metal tools. They were highly skilled craftsmen in leatherwork, wood, pottery, basketry and copper.

ATSAHUACA *Population:* unknown. Language group: Panoan. Only a handful of the Atsahuaca, who include the Yamiaca tribe, survive. They once lived along the various tributaries of the Tambopata and Inambari rivers in Peru, fishing and growing maize as their staple crop, and bananas, sweet manioc, cotton and sugar cane. All crops, except sugar cane, were owned communally by a village. They caught fish by damming streams and introducing a drug to stupefy the fish, and were famed for their prowess as hunters with expertly trained dogs. The Yamiaca, but not the Atsahuaca, had canoes and rafts to transport their goods. While the Atsahuaca had little, simple, lean-to huts built for one family, the Yamiaca built large communal huts: in recent years they slept in hammocks—and even beds— rather than on the floor. The Atsahuaca wore beautiful headdresses made from parrots' feathers and shell ornaments suspended from their noses. Chiefs were highly respected, especially by the Atsahuaca who accorded them many privileges. The sick were treated harshly; they were stamped on and beaten with stinging nettles to drive out the debilitating evil spirits. The dead were buried with all their possessions and some of their crops burnt.

AYMARA *Population:* 600,000. Language group: Aymara. The Aymara live in the Titicaca basin in Peru and Bolivia. They have a history of servitude – first to the Incas and then to the Spanish. Under the Spanish there was the *hacienda* system (only finally abolished in 1953) by which Aymara peasants worked up to six days a week for the landowner in return for a piece of land on which to grow their own crops and raise a few animals. In 1953, the former *hacienda* lands were redistributed to those who worked on them. The Aymara, of whom few have left the villages for work in the towns, live in small, over-populated villages and grow cash crops like onions, potatoes, beans and quinoa. There are also many families living in the hills, herding llamas and sheep. Many farmers work as carpenters or tailors to supplement their incomes. Although traditionally married couples lived with the husband's family until children were born, more recently couples have set up house for themselves much earlier. Children are sent to school for a number of years, but also have to help on the farm and in the fields. When they reach marriage age, a boy and a girl will often elope. Their marriage is later ratified by a church service and a reconciliation with their parents. Although, officially, the Aymara are Catholics, the old deities and worship of natural features survive. Every morning the heads of households in the community hold assemblies to thrash out village issues. To gain political and social status a man must be successful both inside and outside the community. He must be able to entertain, know the right people, speak well in assemblies and sway decisions. Feasts are frequently held to celebrate many different occasions – and it is at the dances that most couples meet. *Chicha*, a maize beer, is the most popular drink and most Aymara still chew coca.
(pages 88-97)

BETOI *Population:* unknown. Language group: Tucano. The Betoi live in the humid, verdant mountains of east Colombia. They are hunters and fishers who travel from one area to another by way of the streams and rivers in dugout canoes, living in small, temporary villages. They cultivate a number of crops like maize and manioc, and pineapples, pimentos, and chili peppers. They hunt tapirs, peccaries, deer, bears, jaguars, and pumas with bows and arrows which are sometimes poisoned. Some of the tribes in the area even hunt snakes. In battle they made so much noise that the Spaniards referred to

their attacks as 'shouts'; but their weapons were effective – arrows, spears and axes. Only the headman wears any kind of clothing and this is made of bark cloth. Some Betoi paint their bodies, both for decoration and for protection against the sun and mosquitoes. They have few crafts apart from making bark cloth, pottery and calabash containers. Their villages are organized into small inter-marrying groups led by headmen. They believe in two main gods, the good Sun-God, and a god of evil. When a man dies the Betoi bury him in the kitchen area of his house with cooking utensils and weapons.

BINTIGWA (see ARHUACO)

CAGABA (see KOGI)

CAMPA *Population:* 20,000-30,000. Language group: Arawak. The Campa live in the south-west part of the Montana region in Peru. Until the 1940s they managed virtually to isolate themselves from civilization. More recently many have taken farm jobs and have learned to speak Spanish as well as their native language. Whereas once they built their houses on hilltops, Campa families now live in villages set in clearings along the river banks. Farming provides most of the food: the yams, peanuts, sweet potatoes, bananas, pineapples, tuber beans, taro, pumpkin, sugarcane, and pepper, and also the barbasco which is used as a poison for fishing. The Campa who live higher up in the Sierra also grow coca and potatoes. Recently the rifle has superseded the bow and arrow for hunting tapirs, boars, deer and monkeys. Their traditional crafts include weaving and spinning, basketry, and making coil pots and calabash containers. The Campa were originally taught how to work metals by Franciscan missionaries, and steel axes have long replaced the old stone ones. With this knowledge they also extracted metal from the mines in the Cerro de la Sal. Their main religious festivals are associated with boys' and girls' puberty rites.
(pages 50-59)

CANARI *Population:* unknown, probably extinct. Language group: Canari (Puruha-Mochica). The tribal identity of the Canari, who lived in the highland regions of southern

133

Ecuador, has been submerged within the mass of Indian tribes that proliferate in Ecuador. They lived in farming villages headed by a chief who often had a large, stone, Inca-style square house with a thatched roof. His followers lived in simpler round huts. Their main crops, cultivated by the women, were potatoes, maize, beans, quinoa, and gourds. The men wove cloth, made clothes, and prepared for war. Spears and spear throwers, clubs and axes were their most effective weapons. The Canari herded and ate llamas, hunted deer and rabbits and fished in some coastal areas. Canari craftsmen made intricate crowns, masks, and toys from copper and gold and made fine pottery. Traditionally, chiefs were allowed more than one wife and many must have had several; other Canari had only one wife. There was a powerful network of alliances between the chiefs of the various villages. Trade was important for both political and economic reasons within these alliances.

CANELO *Population:* 2,000. Language group: Quechua. The Canelo live in the forested north-west Montana area on the borders of Peru and Ecuador. They now live with Dominican missionaries at Canelos and cultivate manioc as their staple crop. Before the missionaries came in 1581 they were warlike cannibals. Since 1581 they have been Christian. Their own language is now forgotten. Traditionally they relied on hunting and fishing for their food. They killed birds and monkeys with blowguns, and fish

with harpoons or nets placed end to end across the mouth of the stream, or by drugging the fish with barbasco. They ate wild fruits and, in season, fat palm grubs and flying ants. Until the missionaries introduced chickens, they kept domesticated animals only as pets, not as stock. They lived in palisaded villages and slept in hammocks or on platforms. Canelo families had three dwellings, one in the communal village hut, a private hut for guests, and a secret one in the bush. The women wore simple wrap-around cotton skirts. They manufactured bark cloth, baskets and pots.

CAQUETIO *Population:* nil. Language group: Arawak. The Caquetio once lived in the Peninsula of Baraguan and the off-shore islands. With the coming of the Spanish—who branded all the Indians in the area as 'Carib' or cannibals, and then sold them off as slaves – the Caquetio fled to take refuge in the jungles around Ele river. Although they lived in coastal areas, the Caquetio were traditionally farmers, growing maize, manioc and sweet potatoes. Their houses, each occupied by several families, were built around the fields to protect the crops. A man could have several wives. The Caquetio had a hereditary chief and under his leadership they ruled over several other tribes; the chief was regarded as almost divine, with powers over nature. At the death of a nobleman, the body was burnt and the bones crushed into a powder which was added to a mixture of *masato* – a fire-water made from *yuca* – and then drunk.

CATIO *Population:* unknown. Language group: Choco. The Catio live in the east of the Atrato valley in Colombia. Their large, well-fortified houses are built off the ground on piles, and accommodate several families. Inside, the Catio have special clay or wooden jars for storing rainwater which runs down bamboo gutters. Their houses are reached by fortified roads. They were once a warlike people: before a battle men would specially cut their hair. Clothes are made of cotton or bark cloth. Traditionally, a man could have as many as twenty wives, and numerous slaves to farm the land. In their curious system of inheritance, the slave who worked longest for his master inherited the dead man's wives and all his property. Today each Catio family has a patch of land on which they cultivate maize, sugar cane and other crops. They no longer keep slaves, but wives are still

subservient to their husbands. A wife is often divorced as her husband tires of her and ceases to find her attractive. Children likewise can be thrown out of the household by their fathers. Shamans who are asked to cure sickness, are also feared for their powers of causing sickness. Although gradually the Catio are being pushed off their land by white farmers and planters, they cling tenaciously to their culture and persistently refuse to adopt a western way of life.

CAYAPA *Population:* 2,500. Language group: Chibcha. The Cayapa are one of the last Indian groups remaining in the north-western lowlands of Ecuador. They live along the many rivers that cut through the rainforest: the rivers are their highways, and the Cayapa are expert at building and navigating their dugout canoes. In their settlements the Cayapa live by fishing, hunting and cultivating crops like plantains, bananas and sugar cane. Each family has its own hut in the middle of its fields. Some keep pigs and chickens. The independent household of grandparents, parents and children is the basic social and economic unit. Politically the Cayapa are led by a chief and various lesser chiefs, who hold their positions from father to son subject to the confirmation of the priest. There are other official posts with Spanish titles, which probably existed long before Spanish names were given to them. Most Cayapa are Christians, and they have built four churches with the help of missionaries; but many traditional and superstitious ceremonies are still performed. At a marriage the chief publicly beats both the man and the woman. On festival days the men wear western style clothes – usually a vest and shorts. Children go naked until they are about eight years old. Since World War II, the boom demand for rubber, balsa wood and bananas has brought a huge expansion of plantation farming in this region. Gradually the Cayapa are being forced away from their river settlements and from their traditional way of life.
(pages 36-43)

CHAKE *Population:* 5,000. Language group: Carib. The Chake are one of the tribes grouped by the Spanish under the name of Motilones – which means 'with cut hair' – who live in Venezuela and Colombia in the Cordillera Oriental, the Sierra de Perija and the eastern side of the Serrania de los Motilones. Most of the other Motilones

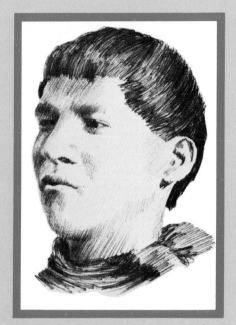

tribes are now extinct or integrated into the *mestizo* population, but the Chake have remained independent and hostile. They are small, almost the size of pygmies; they grow manioc and maize as staple crops, also plantains, sugar cane and bananas. The men hunt with bows and unfeathered reed arrows and plant and clear the fields. Their wives do the harvesting. Although in the past many Motilone tribes built stone and mud houses, the Chake family hut is a simple lean-to. The men wear long cotton tunics and caps, while the women wear loin cloths; often unmarried girls go naked. Babies, however, are wrapped up in long skirt-like clothes. At puberty a girl is secluded in her hut for ten days. Chake chiefs exercise little real authority.

CHANE *Population:* unknown. Language group: Guarani. The Chane live on the eastern slopes of the Bolivian Andes. In the Middle Ages they were conquered by the Guarani (see volume VI) and have ceased, since early this century, to speak their own language. Today they are almost totally integrated into the dominant Guarani culture. The Chane have been proficient farmers since before their conquest and today cultivate cotton, tobacco, 11 varieties of maize, pumpkins, beans, sweet potatoes, manioc, peanuts, and barbary figs. They keep some sheep, cattle, horses and chickens. In the larger rivers, women and children fish with iron hooks. The Chane of the Parapeti River use fishing nets and then shoot the fish with cactus-tipped arrows – their most common

weapon. They kindle fire with steel and flint – although there are references to the fire-drill in Chane mythology. In their oral traditions the Chane recall the names of several female, as well as male, chiefs.

CHANTAQUIRO (see PIRO)

CHIPAYA (see URU-CHIPAYA and pages 98-103)

CHIBCHA *Population:* 850,000. Language group: Chibcha. The Chibcha who, like the Incas, worshipped the sun and made human sacrifices, lived in the high basins of the Cordillera Oriental in Colombia. After their conquest by the Spaniards in 1536, which they ineffectively resisted, their culture, described as of almost equal importance to the Inca culture, began a steady decline, and has made only a small impression on the history of the South American continent. Their political organization was loose so that kingdoms were impermanent, rulers quarrelsome and no large forces could be mobilized against the Spanish. Rebellions in response to Spanish cruelty were hopeless from the start. Villages were often large, with markets every four days. Their circular or square houses were built of cane covered with mud daub. Palaces and temples were large but built in the same way, as the Chibcha did not use stone. Both men and women worked the fields which yielded plenty of food: the main crops were maize and potatoes. Rabbits were their only meat for although deer were prolific in the region, the chief's permission was required to kill them. They traded extensively, worked copper and gold, though less skilfully than other tribes, and made cotton clothes decorated with paint. Men and women wore similar cloth mantles. They rarely used bows and arrows; their principal weapon was the spear and spear thrower. They buried their dead in well-graves up to 40 feet deep. Religious ceremonies involved human sacrifice. In one of these the chief would be smeared with a sticky substance and powdered with gold dust which would finally be washed off by bathing in a sacred lake. This practice was one of the origins of the legend of El Dorado – the Golden Man.

CHIMANE *Population:* 3,000. Language

group: Mosetene. The Chimane live along the Bopi, Quiquibey and Beni rivers in Bolivia cultivating maize, sweet manioc and bananas as staples and recently crops like coffee, rice and onions. To supplement their diet they hunt and are expert fishermen who build weirs in the rivers and catch the fish by poisoning the stream and hauling out the drugged fish. The Chimane who live on mission stations now also dry and store fish. The forest Chimane build only temporary huts, and every village has a central men's hut. The whole Chimane tribe is split into small social and political units, of which the family is the most important. A man may marry as many wives as he can support. After puberty, girls are free to have sexual relations with anyone except close kin. Usually a young girl begins with a trial marriage, later reaffirmed with the birth of a child. The traditional Chimane religion entailed scarification of men. There were also powerful shamans who could influence the spirits. Today most Chimane regard themselves as Christian.

CHIRIGUANO *Population:* 10,000. Language group: Tupi-Guarani. The Chiriguano are descendents of the Guarani (see Volume VI) who migrated from Paraguay to the eastern slopes of the Bolivian Andes and conquered the Chane (*q.v.*) people of the area. They adopted Chane methods of cultivation and now grow maize, beans, sweet potatoes, manioc and peanuts. Men build fences round the fields to keep out wild animals. They supplement their diet in times of shortage with wild fruits, and raise sheep,

cattle, horses, and chickens. Traditionally the Chiriguano lived in large circular communal huts, with an open space in the middle and in villages; today their houses still cluster round a central plaza. They make beautiful pottery and are skilled in weaving wool, making baskets and calabash containers. Their main weapon is the bow. In the past some of the chiefs who controlled the villages would extend their influence over a wide area and be recognized as supreme chiefs. Cannibalism and warfare were common: during the 16th century, the Chiriguano are estimated to have eaten 60,000 Chane. The Chiriguano of today are noted for their custom of bathing several times a day.

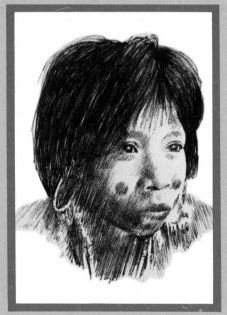

CHOCO *Population:* 5,000. Language group: Chorotegan. The Choco tribes live along the Pacific coast of Colombia farming, fishing, and hunting with varying emphasis according to their location. They hunt many different animals – deer, monkeys and peccaries – with poisoned arrows, and keep domestic animals like chickens, pigs and ducks. Their simple huts are built on piles because of frequent flooding. Their dugout canoes are built for long trips on the rivers; for the Choco are great traders. Men wear loincloths and many ornaments and decorations. Women wear only skirts. Before marriage, husband and wife have a mock fight, and then the wife's father fights her husband. Then the couple live alternately with their respective parents as both men and women have the right to cultivate land in their

father's plots. Households are headed by the eldest male and the village chiefs are only temporary war leaders. Shamans are probably the most powerful members of the community for they practise witchcraft, cure the sick and have the ear of the spirits.

CHONO *Population:* unknown. Language group: unknown. The Chono, who once lived in the hilly islands off the south-west coast of Chile in the Archipielago de los Chons, became almost extinct as an independent group at the end of the last century. Their present-day descendants have merged with other Indian groups and no distinguishable Chono survive. Fish, shellfish (which the women dived for) and seals provided their main diet. They were keen traders and they used canoes as their only transport, and the sea as their only means of communication because of the hilly, thickly forested nature of the island. Before the Europeans arrived they kept only dogs as domesticated animals, but later also kept sheep and goats. Their huts were of simple stick frames covered with either bark, branches or skins. Their canoes were built up of three planks caulked with bark, and although this system was reported to have been efficient, the canoes needed constant bailing. The planks were made without axes, by carefully burning the wood and scraping it smooth with shells and flints. Their political organization is unknown, and the little knowledge we have of their religion tells us only of frenzied rituals and mutilation of their bodies.

COAIQUER *Population:* unknown. Language group: Chibcha. The Pacific coast of Colombia, the home of the Coaiquer, is covered with rainforest similar to that in tropical Amazonia. The Coaiquer are culturally closer to the people of the Amazon than to those of the Andes. Most live as they have always done, preferring a nomadic forest existence to the village life which others have accepted. The forest Coaiquer live in temporary huts and depend for their livelihood on the fruits of the forest, roots, fish and small animals. A man who wishes to marry lives with his bride-to-be for a year to discover whether the match will be successful. If they are not happy together they may part. The Coaiquer control epidemics by isolating the area where disease has developed. They block all paths, destroy all bridges and leave the sick victims behind in the care of someone who is immune. Immunity, they believe, is

gained by chewing coca leaves which contain cocaine.

COLORADO *Population:* 200. Language group: Chibcha. The Colorado are fast losing their identity as a separate tribe, for the colonization of their homeland on the upper parts of the Esmeraldas and Daule rivers in Ecuador, is rapidly drawing them into the plantation system. The Colorado live in the rainforests where traditionally they rely heavily on hunting and fishing, but also extensively cultivate the river lands, mainly with plantains. Their fields are carefully organized and different types of crops are grown at varying distances from their homes. In recent years their agriculture has shifted from purely subsistence farming to growing cocoa trees, cutting balsa wood, rubber tapping and to trade with outside markets. They hunt mostly with shotguns and by stupefying the fish with poison, and pulling them out as they float to the surface. There are no real villages and their houses are often as large as barns. Their religion is a mixture of Catholicism and their own traditional beliefs. They still have shamans who contact and influence both good and evil spirits for the people. Catholic priests perform their marriages and christenings but only after the native ceremonies have also taken place. The Colorado (which means 'red' in Spanish) were so named because of their custom of painting their bodies red.

DIAQUITA *Population:* nil. Language group: Diaquita. The only evidence of the way of life of this group who lived in north-western Argentina is archaelogical. Normally the Diaquita were sedentary farmers, probably cultivating maize and herding llamas, alpacas, and rheas. They used two distinct types of dwelling – one for peaceful and the other for wartime pursuits. Their peacetime houses were square and of dry masonry construction. Their fortified houses were built on the tops of hills. Even a few of the towns were fortified. Warriors wore feathers, silver armbands and engraved chest plates. Their main weapon was the bow and arrow, although they would also use the club in close combat. From their forts they would roll rocks down onto enemy forces. Men, women and children all fought together. The revolutionary Spanish traitor, Bohorquez, taught them to use firearms. They manufactured textiles with llama wool, basketry, ceramics and decorated urns which have been found in burial sites. The most striking examples of their skills in metal work are large ceremonial axes, breast plates and forehead plates.

ESMERALDA *Population:* unknown. Language group: Chibcha. When the Spaniards first explored north-west Ecuador they discovered emeralds; and so they named the people of this area Esmeralda. There is evidence that before the Spanish Conquest these people were ethnically more distinct and spoke a separate language. But by the time of conquest the Esmeralda had been almost completely displaced by colonies of the neighboring Manta (*q.v.*); already they spoke Chibcha, the general language of the area. The Esmeralda lived in coastal villages and were frequently at war with each other. They depended for their livelihood almost entirely on fishing and trade with the interior. They were skilled weavers of cotton cloth and made ornaments in gold and silver, many of them set with emeralds. They were skilled in glazing pottery, and in the construction of dugout canoes. Ear-rings and nose plugs decorated their faces, and for superstitious reasons they also bound their heads into unnaturally elongated shapes.

EUROPEANS see the introduction to the Glossary for discussion of the European strains in the population of South America.

GAYON *Population:* unknown. Language group: Jirajara. Little is known about the Gayon; it is thought that they must now all be integrated with other tribes. The Gayon lived in the Venezuelan Llanos and in the plains and hills surrounding them. Their most interesting cultural trait was their use of earth ovens. Their staple foods were agaves and palms, and the deer and rabbits which they hunted. They had no huts and at night simply slung hammocks between trees.

GUAJIRO *Population:* 50,000. Language group: Arawak. The Guajiro live on the Guajiro peninsula of Colombia and Venezuela. The land is hilly in the north, with vast, dry, infertile plains in the south. Hunting and fishing provide part of the diet for the majority of the people, but in some more fertile areas they grow cocoa, maize, plantains and onions. The hunting Guajiro tend to look down on the agriculturalists. Primarily however, the Guajiro raise and breed cattle. Because of their cattle's need for water and the extended dry seasons, the Guajiro are nomadic. In times of severe drought, they move down to the coast and dig wells, sometimes 30 feet deep, near the shore. Besides cattle, the Guajiro also herd horses, goats, sheep and donkeys. As they regard their cattle as important symbols of wealth, they seldom kill them but drink their milk and make it into cheese. They frequently kill goats and sheep instead for their meat. They trade their animals' skins with Colombian and Venezuelan traders for spirits, ammunition and other western products. During the salt season men and women work the salt deposits and go to the towns and ports to load salt from warehouses to the ships, which enables them to buy still more goods. The Guajiro are industrious and have quickly adapted to the demands and benefits of a cash economy. Their villages are small and temporary, and shelters are often their only houses.
The Guajiro are divided into matrilineal kinship groups called *castas* which may be widely dispersed over a large area. Each has its own territory and a hereditary chief who succeeds to the position through his maternal uncle. The uncle bequeaths all his property to his eldest sister's eldest son. Chiefs have many wives and thus many daughters, each of whom will bring into the chief's family a large bride-price payment in cattle. The Guajiro's religion is officially Catholic, but in practice shamanism is still predominant. At puberty girls may be isolated for as long as two years. After their isolation they may be married, if a high enough bride-price is offered. Every

man who can afford it tries to marry at least two wives.
(pages 14-23)

GUAYUPE *Population:* unknown. Language group: Arawak. At the beginning of this century almost all the people of the Guayupe tribes – who included the Sae and lived in the Llanos de San Juan in Venezuela and Colombia – finally became fully integrated with other groups. They were in the past, keen traders, exchanging their cotton for gold, jewels and other precious objects. Canoes provided the means of travel. They fished and cultivated their staple foods of maize, sweet potatoes and beans; they grew other crops, but only for trade. In their villages the houses, each occupied by several families, centered round a ceremonial hut in the center of plaza. They wore few clothes, if any, but like to wear decorations: women sometimes wore pieces of bark, hung from their waists. Each of their villages had its own headman; there were no higher chiefs. When a headman died, he was cremated and his ashes drunk by the more important people, to bring the dead man back into their lives. Marriages were negotiated with a bride-price and men could have several wives. The Sae had two methods of marriage: one was an annual feast at which everyone danced, followed by general lovemaking when married couples remained with each other, but those who wished to marry could sleep with their proposed spouses. Alternatively, after her puberty rituals a girl could announce which man she wanted as her husband; although the man was not bound to accept. If they were not pregnant within a year of marriage wives often left their husbands going from man to man, if necessary, until they had a child. All the tribes in the area were very war-like and boys' puberty rites were dictated by war-like rituals. Men tested each other by jumping through fires; boys were whipped with nettles and pricked with heated lances to endow them with strength and courage. The Guayupe frequently engaged in witchcraft and sorcery and esteemed and feared their shamans.

HUARPE *Population:* unknown. Language group: Huarpe-Comechingonan. The Huarpe lived in the Mendoza region of central Argentina, east of the Andes. They have become gradually extinct since the time of the Spanish Conquest in the 16th century. They cultivated only one crop, maize, but also relied on hunting rhea, guanaco, deer and aquatic birds. They used canals to irrigate their fields which were often terraced. The arrival of the Spanish brought no innovations, they did no more than improve the existing agriculture. Their houses were of varied construction – some were built on stilts in lakes, others were of reed and mud construction on the plains. Their main means of transport was the reed boat. Pottery was the principal Huarpe craft; their chief weapon was the bow and arrow. Families were organized into landowning groups under a chieftain. The Huarpe god was called Hunuc Huar. When a Huarpe man died his personal belongings and food were buried with him.

HUILLICHE (see ARAUCANIAN)

ICA (see ARHUACO)

INCAS Language group: Quechua. Inca is a group name which covers a large number of tribes. The original Incas were Quechua speakers who lived in the south-eastern Peruvian highlands. Tribes later conquered by the Incas tended to assimilate Inca culture, to the exclusion of their own. In the 15th century, led by Pachacuti Inca Yupaqui and his son Topa Inca, the Inca Empire exploded over the Andes. Both leaders claimed to be descendants of the Sun, the most important symbol in Inca religious life. When Topa Inca died in 1493 Pachacuti's Andean domain ran nearly 2,500 miles from north Ecuador into Chile and covered some 350,000 square miles. The Incas are famous for their intricate goldwork and elaborate weaving. For subsistence they relied on terraced and irrigated cultivation, and very little on hunting and fishing. In mountain areas the main crop was quinoa, and in lower areas maize, beans, peanuts, and squash. They kept llamas, alpacas, dogs, guinea pigs and ducks. Men worked copper and gold and women made fabrics and pots. Inca towns had massive public buildings. Most of their technological achievements were grand-scale copies of ideas from earlier civilizations. Most people lived in square stone houses with thatched roofs. The Inca political system was headed by an absolute divine king and was subdivided into a territorial organization with a hierarchy of bureaucrats. There were

no written records, despite the advanced technology, and history was preserved through narrative poems and genealogies. The empire began to crumble with the Spanish Conquest of Cuzco in 1533.

JIRAJARA *Population:* unknown. Language group: Arawak. The Jirajara are remembered by history, but their descendants have long ceased to be an independent group. Only a few Indians, living to the north-west of Lake Maracaibo in Venezuela can claim some form of descent from the Jirajara. Their homeland was in the Venezuelan mountain states of Falcon, Lara, and Zulia. Most of the tribe were killed in the wars of the Spanish Conquest, or captured, branded as cannibals and sold as slaves. Although most of their villages were built on lake shores, they relied more on farming for their livelihood than on fishing. Their staple crops were maize, manioc, and sweet potatoes, grown on their own plantations. Houses, built on piles, faced each other along a wide street. Men and women had simple clothes, covering little more than the genitals. They moved about, across the lakes and along the streams in dugout canoes; and once 'pacified' they became cargo handlers for the Spanish. Politically the Jirajara were under a tribal war chief, but also divided into sub-tribes, each with its own chief. They were war-like and fiercely resisted the Spanish before being totally subjugated. An important element in the Jirajara religion was the offering of a 10 year old girl to the Sun. The girl was bought from her mother and then offered as a wife to the Sun to obtain rain; the girl was then decapitated. Shamans were very powerful, dealing with the spirits and healing the sick.

KOGI (Cagaba) *Population:* 2,000. Language group: Arhuaco. The Kogi inhabit the Sierra Nevada de Santa Marta in northern Colombia, a mountainous area of about 5,000 square miles. For hundreds of years, largely due to a disruptive missionary influence on their traditional life, the Kogi have been retreating into less accessible mountain areas of their tribal territory. However their population remains stable. The Kogi traditionally follow a seasonal migration, meeting periodically at temples in the highlands for religious ceremonies and festivals. During the colonial period permanent settlements were imposed on the Kogi to make tax collection easier – but today those same villages are largely deserted. Kogi

families now devote much of their time to cultivating sugar cane, cotton, tobacco and coca, some of which is traded. Hunting and fishing are of negligible importance. While other tribes in the area keep pigs, sheep, turkeys, chickens and dogs, the Kogi keep only oxen as domesticated animals. Horses are rare. Kogi houses preserve a pre-Columbian design: round with grass-thatched, conical roofs. While the women use cotton and wool to make cloth, men make pots for cooking, fermenting sugar cane wine and toasting coca leaves. The Kogi play many musical instruments in their festivals: drums, flutes, trumpets, and rattles. Their religion involves many spirits, above all ancestor spirits.
(pages 44-49)

LAMA *Population:* less than 1,000. Language group: Quechua. The Lama live in the Montana area of northern Peru to the west of the Maranon River. They now dress in the Spanish style, having lost much of their ethnic identity and culture. Once they hunted with spears, blowguns and darts poisoned with liana sap. Now they grow bananas, plantains, maize, yams, sweet manioc, peanuts, sweet potatoes, beans, pumpkins, egg-plants and sugarcane. They catch fish with harpoons, spears and bows, and trap them and drug them in dams. Their houses are rectangular, with thatched roofs. They make baskets and pots and enjoy playing musical instruments including drums, panpipes and flutes. Tobacco and coca are their main narcotics. In 1830 they were recorded as being Catholic, but their conversion to this faith probably occurred much earlier.

LECO *Population:* under 500. Language group: Leco. The few remaining Leco live on the eastern slopes of the Bolivian Andes along the Kaka River. When first contacted in the early part of the 17th century they defeated the Spanish and killed the sergeant who attempted to conquer them. A number of Franciscan missions were set up in the area but the Leco, hostile after their first encounter with the Spanish, destroyed the most important one. Maize and bananas were probably their staple foods. They caught fish with bow and arrows or by drugging them. Today the rivers are still important to Leco economy, and balsa rafts, held together with palm spikes, are the chief form of transport for both people and goods.

MANTA *Population:* unknown. Language group: Puruha-Mochica. The Manta are the coastal trading and fishing people of Ecuador although they have almost completely lost their identity and culture. They are sometimes referred to as the Liga de Mercaderos – the League of Traders. Once they lived in large villages in houses made of cane or wood and covered with thatch. Food came from a number of different sources: maize, manioc, and potatoes were cultivated by women, while men hunted deer and game birds. Ducks, llamas and other animals were domesticated. The Manta wore gold and silver earrings and nose plugs and their faces were often tatooed. They transported goods by huge balsa rafts which could carry 20 people and 30 tons of merchandise: wool cloth, embroidered blankets, silver and gold, and some emeralds. Trading trips were also ceremonial as quantities of red beads were carried for ceremonial exchange. The Inca are believed to have been involved in this trade. When a man died he was buried with living women, precious objects and food. The sun, the moon, and the sea were sacred to the Manta.

MAPUCHE (see ARAUCANIAN)

MESTIZO The *mestizos* are those people who are of partly Indian blood. They are not a tribal group. In the general socio-political hierarchy of South America they are regarded as inferior to the whites and superior to the Indians. The large majority of *mestizos* are peasant farmers and laborers. They are found all over South America and form the largest population group in the continent. **(See introduction to the Glossary.)**

MOSETENE (see CHIMANE)

MOTILONE (see CHAKE)

NOANAMA (see CHOCO)

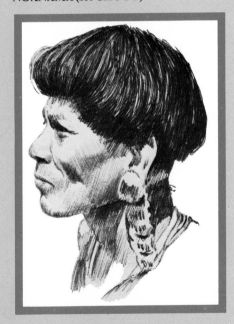

ONA *Population:* under 50. Language group: Chon. A tall, powerfully built people the Ona live on Tierra del Fuego off the very southern tip of South America. Their members have been steeply reduced over the last hundred years by disease, feud, and by seekers and ranchers who invaded the island in the 1880s

and attempted to exterminate them. In this wind- and rain-swept land the Ona lived simply. They wore little clothing except a mantle of skin. They lived entirely from wild food as no plants or animals (other than the dog) were domesticated. They ate guanaco, eels, geese, mussels, cormorants, seals, whales, limpets, crabs, ducks and sometimes foxes, fungi, berries and grass seeds. But they never ate dogs, which they used for hunting, as well as bows and arrows and snares; they fished with spears, and nets. They made houses of guanaco hides sewn over a conical wooden frame and used large huts, made of turf, for ceremonial purposes. Although the Ona are reputed to have travelled by sea, there is no evidence of how they did so. Their manufactures included string and twine, baskets, stone-tools, and skin containers. Children of different sexes were kept apart from an early age and premarital sex relations were uncommon. Both boys and girls could marry the person of their choice except for certain blood relations. Divorce was rare. Each family was an independent political and economic unit, although there were wider groupings of kin which owned territory on which their members had the right to hunt at any time. There were 39 such territories each of which supported from 40 to 120 people. Although hunting disputes sometimes turned into fights, there were no large-scale battles.
(pages 110-119)

OTAVALO *Population:* 34,000. Language

13

group: Quechua. The Otavalo live in Ecuador, in a pleasant, fertile valley high in the Andes about seventy miles north of Quito. When the Incas invaded their valley in the 15th century and lived there in peaceful domination, the Otavalo assimilated a lot of Inca culture. They are often called the aristocrats of Ecuador's Indians partly because of their Inca descent but more because of their adaptation to a modern economy. Owing to increasing pressure on their lands they have found ways of getting a living other than farming. Trading is the most dynamic. Otavalo merchants sell their woven clothes and ponchos in the streets and markets of Ecuador, Colombia, Chile and Brazil and as far afield as Mexico and the USA. Otavalo can be distinguished from *mestizos* and other Indians by their clothes. Men wear heavy white cotton shirts over loose mid-calf length pants. Over these they wear dark-blue woolen ponchos. On their heads they wear wide brimmed felt hats and on their feet cloth sandals with rope soles. Women wear bright, heavily embroidered cotton blouses and two long heavy woolen skirts. Over their blouses they wear short woolen shawls tied in a knot and they adorn themselves with strings of gold colored beads. **(pages 60-67)**

PAEZ *Population:* 500. Language group: Talamanca-Barbacoa. The Paez live in southern Colombia, on the eastern slopes of the Cordillera Central. Although only a few are left they have kept their identity. Their staple food is the potato; other crops include manioc, maize, sweet potatoes, bananas, guavas, avocados, pineapples and passion fruit. Today they increasingly grow wheat, coffee, and sugar cane, from which they make an alcoholic drink *guarapo*, and they keep chickens, turkeys, pigs, dogs, horses, and cows. Normally work is done on a family basis but for large-scale maize or coffee planting communal labor is used. The Paez build bridges, which vary from a simple vine to a solid log structure with a roof, over the deep gorges and valleys. They make baskets, ropes and coil pots and use calabashes as containers. In the past they worked gold and copper. Long heavy spears were once their main weapons, but today they use guns, clubs, machetes and blow-guns. Each community comprised several families under a chief who would unite them for some agricultural work and for war.

PANTANGORO The Pantangoro, of whom the Amani are a sub-division, have been extinct for several centuries but their history is spectacular as for many years these tribes were believed to represent all the evils of primitive Indian life. These fierce, warlike tribes lived in the eastern forest of the Cordillera Central of Colombia where they grew maize as their staple food. The Amani were cannibals in the fullest sense for they roasted or barbecued whole bodies, or ground the bones into powders to add to drinks. They stored human flesh in large quantities; the delicacies being considered the hands, feet, and bowels. Their independent villages were heavily fortified with palisades, deep trenches, secret pits and traps, and built in the most inaccessible places. The powers of their headmen and chiefs were limited except in war. They obtained wives by exchanging sisters and marriage to one sister gave sexual access to all the wife's other sisters. For the Pantagoro marriages were easily broken. The Amani, however, treated an adulterous wife harshly: all the men in the locality would be allowed to rape her before leaving her to starve to death. To make children brave and tough they would be taken to bloody corpses and made to push sticks into the wounds. Poison for use on arrow tips was concocted by boiling snakes, from tree sap and where possible, from men's testicles and menstrual blood. The fumes sometimes killed those preparing the poison. Shamans among the Pantangoro were killed if the patient failed to live. They believed in life after death.

PANZALEO (see QUITO)

PASTO *Population:* 50,000. Language group: Tucanoan. The Pasto live on the western borders of Colombia and Ecuador. Their houses are made of poles stuck into the ground, covered with palm leaves and plastered with mud. They sleep on beds fastened to the walls. Each house has its own plot of land where the family grow for their own consumption potatoes, barley, and maize. Most families also have a flower garden. They keep oxen and sheep which they value so much that they treat them almost as pets. Men wear a shirt, pants and poncho. Women wear a shawl with woolen skirts. Both sexes habitually wear felt hats: the old woolen felt hats are said to last for more than 100 years. Tools are all of colonial origin – the horse-drawn plow, machete, and shovel. The Pasto do some wool weaving. Many now labor in the city.

PICUNCHE (see ARAUCANIAN)

PIRO *Population:* 5,000. Language group: Arawak. The Piro, who include the Chantaquiro (named after their black stained teeth) occupy the south-west Montana area in Peru adjacent to the Campa (*q.v.*). Before the Conquest the Piro are thought to have been in contact with the Incas. After the Conquest they retained their ethnic identity more or less intact until the beginning of this century. Throughout, they welcomed missionaries, primarily as a source of metal tools. In the early 1900s many of them died in slavery, working on rubber plantations. Today they are farmers who produce sweet manioc, bananas, and some coca and supplement their diet by killing fish and game, tapirs, boars, deer, and monkeys. Although they keep chickens, they eat only the eggs. In their houses, about 20 feet long and 18 feet high, they sleep on rectangular platform beds. A fire is kept constantly burning. Both men and women wear the *cushma*: a loose-sleeved tunic made of cotton or bark cloth. They make netted bags of cotton cloth and crude pottery. They file wood with a rasp made of the dried tongue of the *payshi* fish. Their main weapons, which they shoot left-handed, are bows and arrows.

PUELCHE *Population:* under 50. Language group: Puelche. The Puelche originally occupied a large portion of central Argentina, around and north of the Colorado River until the 18th century, when smallpox occurred which few survived. In the 18th century their staple food was horse meat and they ate lice. They had no agriculture and only one domesticated animal – the dog. They probably acquired horses in the early 18th century. They used horse-skin to make clothes and, over a wooden frame, to make traditional huts. They had few crafts and made flint tools. Most men had one wife but prominent men had two or three. They lived in small bands under a headman, whose authority derived solely from his power to command, his use of oratory, and his skill as a warrior. Their main weapons were the bow, lance, sling *bolas*, and lasso. The Puelche were continually at war with each other, wearing armour made of horse hide and fighting with the lance rather than bows and arrows, which were considered cowardly in warfare.

QUECHUA *Population:* 3 million. Language group: Quechua. All the inhabitants of the Andes who speak Quechua are described as Quechua people. They are descendants of the ancient Inca civilization who, since the warfare and disease that followed the Spanish Conquest when there were 6 million Incas, have declined in numbers. Their culture has largely been submerged beneath Spanish culture: many are Roman Catholics; many crops and livestock have been imported and transformed their means of subsistence, although often their motive in adopting them was less to modify their own existence than to pay the heavy tribute demanded by the Spanish. They certainly have not embraced innovations wholesale. In the 19th century highland Peruvians still ate maize, grasses, alpaca and llama meat, quinoa flour and potatoes. And many European crops – wheat, figs, pomegranates, quinces and olives would only grow in certain areas. But cattle quickly became numerous and they bred horses wherever possible. Their traditional crop, tobacco, they only used medicinally; the Spanish used the bulk of the crop. Coca is today as it always was, the principal Indian narcotic. Acceptance of Spanish culture became identified with social rank: Indian nobles wore full European dress while lesser people wore traditional outfits, although the standard felt hat commonly identified as Indian wear, is of Spanish origin. The crafts of colonial life included wood, silver and bronze working. The Quechua simplified the Inca political organization. The traditional pyramid of authority was destroyed when the

Indians came under Spanish authority and paid regular tribute. Spanish influence quickly brought Christianization. Spanish churches, some of which were built by Indians for Indian use, are common in many areas. Colonial mining technology organized Indians into work groups and vast numbers died during this exploitation. These Indian groups placed under Spanish command were called *encomiendas*. Warfare in the colonial period was confined to rebellion. Today those Quechua who do not live – as many do – in towns, are peasant farmers growing potatoes, maize, barley, broad-beans, quinoa and wheat on a rotation basis, and herding sheep, llamas, and alpacas. Their communities are called *ayllus*, and a highland *ayllu* will often own land many miles away in the lowland valleys. Thus a highland community will have access also to the crops which can only be grown in the valleys. Weaving cotton and wool in a variety of designs is their most important craft. They also make basketry, rope and cord, woodwork, hats and pottery. Their houses are rectangular and made of stone and adobe. Each community has a hierarchy of officials.
(pages 68-79)

QUIMBAYA *Population:* extinct. Language group: unknown. The central Cauca valley of the northern Andes in Colombia was the home of the Quimbaya. Evidence of their way of life is archaeological as the ancient Quimbaya are now totally extinct. Most remains of Quimbaya culture came from graves which have been excavated. They worked gold objects with great skill but little silver was available and copper was

rare. They made distinctive ceramics and many stone tools: axes, beads and grindstones.

QUITO *Population:* unknown. Language group: Quechua. In the past the Panzaleo and Quito, of whom only a few survive, lived close to each other in central Ecuador. They were very similar and maintained such close contact that they are thought of as one group. They quickly lost their native language in Inca and colonial times, as this area was an important administrative center and the general language was Quechua. Farming in this fertile region, provided most of the food: they grew maize, potatoes, beans, quinoa, and cotton, and sold surplus produce in markets. Land was owned privately and a man had only to stake his claim to clear and cultivate a plot. The Quito also hunted for game which proliferated in the area. Women worked in the fields. Men were the craftsmen and produced cloth and clothes, and for fighting they used spears and clubs. The Panzaleo were particularly expert with the spear thrower and sling. Chiefs, who were important and lived in large houses, were often much richer than their followers and owned much gold and jewelry. Ordinary people lived in small, scattered settlements of houses made of mud with thatched roofs. The Quito for whom hair cutting was one of the most severe punishments, second only to death, never voluntarily cut their hair.

SAE (see GUAYUPE)

___

SAHA (see ARHUACA)

___

SPANISH The immense contribution of Spanish blood to the peoples of South America is discussed in the introduction to the Glossary.

___

TAIRONA The Tairona once occupied the area inhabited by the Kogi (*q.v.*). They lived in circular stone huts and made stone and clay pots. They used copper and gold to make beads, rings, plaques and pendants.

___

TEHUELCHE *Population:* 350. Language group: Chon. The Tehuelche live in southern Argentina. They once lived mainly on guanaco, armadillos and quan meat. They never cultivated crops but supplemented their diet with wild plants, roots, seeds and fruits. They had no domesticated animals other than the dog, which they used for hunting. When the horse was introduced around 1725 it became part of their diet. They never established permanent dwellings but sometimes used caves and simple skin windbreaks for shelter, or more commonly a twin-roomed skin tent known as a *toldo*. They rarely lived more than twenty to a camp. Although they later used horses their only transport was originally by means of a crude

type of coracle. Their only craft was a primitive kind of pottery until the coming of the horse which led to the development of lassoo plaiting and in the 19th century they began to work in silver. Their chief hunting weapon, the bow and arrow, was replaced by the *bolas* and the lassoo. In battle they wore hide armor. Wife-beating, common in many South American Indian societies, was very rare among the Tehuelche.

___

TEPQUI *Population:* unknown. Language group: Panoan. Little is known about the Tepqui of the central Peruvian Montana. They seem to have blended with the neighboring tribes. They have been described as Canoe Indians. They wore their hair in bundles down the back. Men had only one wife and a newly married couple set up an independent household.

___

TIMOTE *Population:* extinct. Language group: Timote. The Timote, about whom little is known, were a warlike people who lived south-west of Lake Maracaibo in Venezuela. The only surviving Indians of this area are the Chake (q.v.).

___

TUNEBO *Population:* 1,800. Language group: Chibcha. The Tunebo live in Venezuela in the north-eastern Andes to the south of Lake Maracaibo, close to the Colombian border. They keep no animals and rely for their livelihood on agriculture, growing maize as the main crop by shifting cultivation. They supplement their diet by hunting, fishing and the gathering of wild fruits. When a man marries – usually a girl from the same village – he makes a small payment to his bride's parents and sometimes works for them to prove himself a good husband. A man usually has two or more wives who live together in the same dwelling. Tunebo villages tend to be permanent settlements of 100-200 people. The Tunebo make a potent snuff (*parica*) from the seed of the Piptadenia tree.

___

URU-CHIPAYA *Population:* 1,200. Language group: Uru. The Uru traditionally inhabited the area round Lake Titicaca on the border of Bolivia and Peru. Over the years, they have spread down to the coast so that today there are clearly distinguished coastal

and highland Uru. There are about 1,000 left in the coastal region but less than 100 in the Titicaca area. In both places they are surrounded by the Aymara. The highland Uru fish on Lake Titicaca and the River Desaguedero with V-shaped nets and sometimes with spears. The reed-swamps abound in water-hens, ducks, geese, heron and gulls, which they catch with slings and *bolasses*. Sometimes they camouflage themselves and catch birds by hand. But for a few sheep, cows and llamas, they keep few livestock. The few potatoes they grow are frozen and dried – the origin of the process by which modern freeze-dried instant coffee is made. Their houses are oval or rectangular and made of turf blocks with reed-thatched roofs. Their boats are made of totora reed and are superbly designed for use in shallow, narrow swampways. Men make grass ropes and women spin llama wool. Their musical instruments, of Aymara origin, include open-ended flutes, double panpipes, and the drum. They trade dried salted fish and reed mats for potatoes, coca, which they chew, thread, quinoa, wooden poles, metal objects, medicines and dyes. Uru worship *Pachamama*, the earth goddess.
(pages 98-103)

___

WELSH See the introduction to the Glossary for a discussion of this European strain in the population of South America.
(pages 124-129)

___

YAHGAN *Population:* 1 or nil. Language group: Yahgan. The Yahgan, all but one of whom now have some mixed blood, live along the Beagle channel of Tierra del Fuego and in other islands at the very tip of South America. Their numbers were diminished largely in the 1880s by measles, typhoid, whooping cough, and smallpox. Despite this extreme cold of the climate, with frequent snow and ice, they went almost naked, protected by a layer of fat: the introduction of clothes by visiting well-wishers and civilizers, led frequently to pneumonia. The Yahgan eat many natural foods: mussels, seals, fish, porpoises, gulls, birds, eggs, whales, limpets, crabs, sea urchins, geese, penguins, cormorants, otters, guanaco, ducks, berries, wild celery and wild parsnips. They have no domesticated plants and keep no animals other than the dog. Their main weapons are the spear, harpoon, club and sling. They hunt seals and whales with spears and harpoons, gather mussels by hand, club or spear birds and catch otters with dogs. In times of famine they eat foxes. They live in temporary settlements of beehive or cone shaped huts covered with grass and move around by canoe. Their manufactured products include plant fibers for sewing and rope-making, bone awls and needles, and they weave baskets and prepare seal skins. There is no higher authority or organized larger group than the family. The Yahgan had a strong sense of, and vigorously defended, their own territory.
(pages 120-123)

YURACARE *Population:* 1,000. Language group: Yuracare. Yuracare territory originally covered a large area of tropical forest at the foot of the Andes stretching west from Santa Cruz in Bolivia. The surviving Yuracare still live in the forest fishing, hunting and farming, growing manioc, maize and bananas as staples and sweet potatoes, gourds, watermelons, pineapples, cayenne pepper, cotton and some tobacco. Once Yuracare farming was embedded in ritual. They went to the fields in special dress, observing certain taboos and playing music. A good hunter was an important man. He would successfully kill jaguars and other animals with bows and arrows and various traps. The Yuracare did not eat domesticated animals. Their houses were just roofs on poles. In the past each village had a special men's house which women were forbidden to enter. They used to cross rivers by floating across on a log but recently they have become proficient canoe builders. Their manufactures include bark cloth, baskets, nets, spun cloth, pots and wood carvings. The bow and arrow is still their main weapon.

All population figures are approximate

YAMIACA (see ATSAHUACA)